IT'S THE INCOME STUPID

THE 7 SECRETS OF
A STRESS-FREE RETIREMENT

PHILIP ROMERO AND RIAAN NEL

Post Hill Press
posthillpress.com

Published in the United States of America

CONTENTS

Acknowledgments v
Preface vii
The 7 Secrets xi

PART I: You Are Smart, But the World Has Changed   1

CHAPTER 1 The Last and Longest Lap 3

CHAPTER 2 The Lopsided Mountain of Retirement Planning 15

CHAPTER 3 The Accumulation Phase: Conventional
and Unconventional Wisdom. 24

CHAPTER 4 The New Normal 41

CHAPTER 5 What the New Normal Means for Your Investments 48

PART II: Decumulation: The Envelopes Approach   51

CHAPTER 6 The Envelopes Approach. 53

CHAPTER 7 Envelopes 0 and 1: Safe Assets 67

CHAPTER 8 Envelope 3: Growth and Inflation Hedging 79

CHAPTER 9 Envelope 2: Medium Term Spending, Moderate Risk Assets . 86

PART III: A Guide to Investment Choices   91

CHAPTER 10 Traditional Options I: Savings Accounts,
Money Market Funds, CDs, Bonds, and
Bond Mutual Funds (Envelopes 1 and 2). 93

CHAPTER 11 Traditional Options II: Stocks and Stock Mutual Funds 98

CHAPTER 12 Traditional Options III: Annuities (Envelopes 1 and 2) . . . 104

CHAPTER 13 Other Insurance Products: Secondary Market Annuities
and Viaticals (Envelopes 2 and 3) 132

CHAPTER 14 Dividend Stocks and Dividend Mutual Funds (Envelope 3) 134

CHAPTER 15 Pass-Through Alternative Investments: REITs, MLPs,
and BDCs (Envelope 3) 137

CHAPTER 16 Traded vs. Nontraded? (Envelope 3). 146

CHAPTER 17 Other Hybrid Equity/Debt Investments:
Preferred Stock, Warrants, and Convertible Preferreds
(Envelope 2 and Envelope 3). 165

CHAPTER 18 Other Alternative Investments: Hedge Funds and
Private Equity (Envelope 3) 167

CHAPTER 19 Inflation Hedges: Precious Metals and Commodities
(Envelope 3) 171

CHAPTER 20 International Investments (Envelope 3) 174

CHAPTER 21 Option Strategies for Income and Hedging;
Buy/Write Funds (Envelope 2 and Envelope 3) 176

PART IV: Sleeping Well   181

CHAPTER 22 Being Stress-Free: Jorge and Lita Rios' Financial Life
Trajectory 183

CHAPTER 23 Do You Need a Financial Advisor? The Truth About
Financial Advice 189

CHAPTER 24 Recovery. 205

CHAPTER 25 For 20-, 30- and 40-somethings 211

CHAPTER 26 Conclusion. 216

RESOURCES 223

ACKNOWLEDGMENTS

Many people helped make this book a reality. Some were sounding boards for the ideas and concepts we discuss in the book. Others read chapters and provided their invaluable inputs. We want to thank the following individuals: Robert Fix, Leslie Warren, Jeff Walters, Heath Carpenter, Geoff Webb, Lita Flores-Romero, Brian Nickerson, Hope Nel and Brian Cowles. A special thanks goes to Jeff Savage, Certified Financial Planner™ and Melba Detlefsen. We also like to thank Debra Englander who guided us through the labyrinth of the publishing industry. This book might not exist without her help.

PHILIP ROMERO

I have been blessed with a variety of role models, none of whom are responsible for the idiosyncratic ways I have integrated their lessons. George Shultz demonstrated that thought and action can be mutually reinforcing, and Pete Wilson leads by example. My wife, Lita Flores-Romero, never gave voice to what must have been her first thought: *"Oh, no: another book…"* Because she actively thinks about many of the issues addressed herein, she was a fount of great ideas. Several chapters only exist at her suggestion. Brian and Ann Nickerson, also active retirement thinkers, let me impose on friendship and provided detailed comments that have made this less abstract and more practical. Of course, while all of these helpmates influenced this product, the responsibility rests with the authors. Even for the gratuitous insult in the book's title.

RIAAN NEL

I want to thank my family for their support in writing this book. My little girl, Mischa, who would come into my office and "write" her own books on scrap paper while I worked. My wife, Hope, listening to me talk about the concepts we used in the book like they were the most interesting topics in the world! My mom, Sandra, for always believing in me. My not so little girl, Roo, making sure I'm fed while working late at night. My almost adult, Sky, for keeping my life interesting. I love all of you.

PREFACE

Congratulations. After working for your entire adult life you have begun preparing for the next life stage—retirement. Your simple act of anticipating the inevitable puts you ahead of many Americans. But as you may have found out already, major transitions impose increased stress, even when the transition is planned and/or happy. This new stage of your life may last for decades, long enough to merit careful planning. You need to focus on the important questions.

Joe Hearn is a financial planner who hosts a website that we recommend (www.intentionalretirement.com). It distills retirement planning to the core essentials, which he captures in three questions. We list them below, along with our own interpretation; we've added a fourth question that pervades much of retirement planning.

1. Where do I want to live?

For your working life your location was driven by your job. In retirement, when your income will come from other sources, you are free to live wherever you wish. You'll have macro options based on your preferences about climate, politics, urbanization (city, country, or suburbs) and proximity to family. Many people move to milder climates, states with lower state taxes, or expatriate out of North America altogether. You also have micro options, such as the type of dwelling. It need not be a detached house; it could be an apartment, a townhouse, or a unit in a retirement community.

Choice is challenging and stressful. Many retirees will live in at least two dwellings; while they are still independent, in a setting they choose, and later in a care community (or with relatives) when they no longer can be independent. They may also split their time among more than one domicile while still independent, since no place can meet all desires. For example, they may move overseas, but spend a month each year visiting the grandkids.

2. What do I want to do?

Too many retirees know far more about what they do *not* want to do: work. But your retirement may last for decades. For most folks, fishing or playing golf can only absorb you for so long. The last stage of your active life is probably your last opportunity to find your purpose. If you can choose when you retire, do it when you have a goal you seek, not merely a burden you wish to escape.

3. Who do I want to do it with?

You may love the people you associate with, or you may not. Retirement provides everyone with new choices. Some may be thrust upon you, like a boomerang child (or aged parent) living in your basement, or a spouse who leaves you soon after the kids move out. But others require reflection. If your job was boring, are you ready to explore new intellectual frontiers? With more interesting friends? Or are you content reading trashy novels and watching daytime TV? Do crowds excite or repel you? Do you need the energy of a city, or the tranquility of seclusion? Once you are free to choose your location, you are also free to choose your human surroundings.

Through our actions each of us answered these questions in earlier stages of our lives, perhaps unconsciously. The difference about retirement is that we have more options (and consequently more stress), and we have greater self-knowledge.

To these considerations we add one more unavoidable question:

4. Will I have enough money?

This question often crowds out the others, because far too many Americans have prepared their finances poorly; and because financial advice is much more lucrative than life coaching. If your answer to this question isn't satisfactory, the other three questions matter little. Money allows choice, so insufficient money means limited options.

In our grandparents' era retirement was simpler: it was shorter (years, not decades so your money did not need to last long), and more predictable (because they expected a secure pension that would not be eroded by inflation). Today those premises have completely changed, and all retirees ask themselves if their money will last as long as they will. Ideally, you and your money will expire simultaneously (unless leaving a financial legacy is important to you).

The trouble, of course, is that the key elements of your planning problem are unknowable. You can estimate how much you will spend, but you can only guess at how long you will need to spend it, and how fast your investments will grow to provide the needed funds.

If you have picked up this book, chances are that you have been conscientious about financially preparing for retirement. You know roughly what you will receive in Social Security and any pensions; you've guessed at the amount you will need to spend each year in retirement; you have guesstimated your "number" (the amount you need to have accumulated to cover what SS and pensions won't); and you have saved diligently, putting the power of compounding to work for you. You have a general idea of the answer to this question.

But your goal while you accumulate is straightforward—to amass as much as you can. Once you no longer have a paycheck you are subject to new uncertainties. Your challenge is to organize the money you have accumulated so that it meets your needs, for as long as you have needs.

As the questions above illustrate, not all retirement stress is financial. But "good stress" of having choices is qualitatively different from the "bad stress" that comes from not having enough money. This book will devote itself exclusively to the fourth, financial question. We want to help you eliminate your greatest stressor, so you have the happy problem of addressing the other three questions.

THE 7 SECRETS

1. Don't decrease stocks *too much* as your investing time horizon shortens, and *increase them later*! (Chapter 3)

2. The 4% withdrawal guideline may cause you to *run out of money*! (Chapters 1 and 5)

3. It's the **income**, stupid! (Chapter 2)

4. *Sequence of returns* can devastate your nest egg. (Chapter 3)

5. It's about *correlation*, not *diversification*. (Chapter 3)

6. The *Envelopes*, please. (Chapter 6)

7. You will need *advice*, and it will be *conflicted*. (Chapter 23)

PART I

YOU ARE SMART, BUT THE WORLD HAS CHANGED

CHAPTER 1

The Last and Longest Lap

Americans are sleepwalking their way to their golden years. According to the Employee Benefit Retirement Institute, only one in four have saved at least $100,000, half have less than $25,000, and one in three have saved *nothing at all* for retirement.

Pensions are a distant memory for more than 80% of the population. Social Security will only provide a subsistence income, by design. In the real world, to generate $50,000 a year in income once you no longer earn it through your work—so that you can retire—will require more than $1 million in assets. (We will explain this below so that you can make your own estimate.) Unless you are the beneficiary of a generous rich relative, those assets only came because you saved some of your earnings every year and invested them for growth.

For those who suffer any of the many self-inflicted financial wounds of the American middle class—too much debt; living paycheck to paycheck; no cushion for financial emergencies; expenses that rise faster than their incomes—there are many good personal finance books to help you climb out of your hole and clean up your act so you don't repeat your mistakes. (And if you are young, we urge you to read a few of these so that you can avoid sabotaging your financial future as many of your elders did theirs.)

But *you* are smart. You have diligently saved and patiently invested. You "bought and held" a diverse portfolio of stocks—probably in indexed mutual funds. You aren't relying on some miracle, or on confiscating the earnings of young workers via high taxes, to fund your retirement.

However, chances are that you aren't prepared for two epochal changes. One has already crept in unnoticed, and another you may not have faced. The first is that investment markets' holiday from history (and volatility) in the late 20th century has ended. We explain the "new normal" of slower economic growth, and greater oscillations between deflation and inflation, in Part III. Greater volatility is a scourge of retirees. You will need new strategies to manage in the new normal.

The second change is more personal and completely inevitable: Some day you will stop working. It may be by choice, or it may be forced on you by poor health or a poor economy. But for the remainder of your (hopefully long) life, you will be reliant on the assets you accumulated when working to fund your spending when you no longer work. Many smart wealth accumulators have given little thought to the decumulation phase of their life. (This is often called the "distribution" phase, but we will use "distribution" in a narrower way later, pertaining to tax requirements.)

Many of the principles that guided you in the long accumulation phase of your life need to be modified in the possibly equally long decumulation phase. The new normal investing environment makes this shift in perspective absolutely essential. This book is a guide to this new paradigm.

Retirement Facts of Life

When benefit programs such as Social Security (and its European analogues) were enacted in the late 19th and early 20th centuries, "retirement" was an unknown concept. Average lifespans to age 67 barely surpassed Social Security's beginning age (65) to receive payments.

In the intervening century, advances in medicine and nutrition have extended lifespans by about one year for each passing decade. A worker who retires in her 60s can expect on average about 20 years of further life, with a significant chance of 30 years or more.

In reaction, employers who had used lifetime pensions as means of attracting and retaining workers realized that longer lifespans were making those pensions unaffordable. Over the three decades from the 1980s through the 2000s, corporate pension plans became an endangered species. Today, only one in five workers can expect one. Pensions are concentrated among government workforces, so they are all but nonexistent in the private sector.

Smart investors know all this and realize that they must accumulate assets to a level needed to provide the income they want once they no longer earn income through work. But while this is an answerable question, it cannot be a purely mathematical exercise, because there are three major elements that are unknowable:

- ▶ How long you will live—you do not want your assets to run out before you do.
- ▶ What rate of growth you should assume in those assets, to generate the income you need.
- ▶ What the trajectory sequence of those returns will be as shown later—the same *average* return produces a very different picture if you retire at the end of a bull market vs. at the beginning.

The 4% Rule

Smart investors have clamored for a simple rule of thumb that can be used to set a target for the assets they must accumulate, that is, their "number" and the rate at which they can decumulate (spend them down) in retirement. In the early 1990s, Southern California financial planner Bill Bengen offered an answer. Bengen examined a generic "balanced" portfolio of 50% stocks and 50% bonds to determine how much could be withdrawn each year under a wide range of historical market conditions.

Large charitable institutions such as foundations have faced this challenge throughout history. They invest their endowments to produce enough growth to at least compensate for inflation. To maintain their tax-exempt status, they are required to spend at least 5% of their endowments each year. But endowments have different challenges than retirees. First, most are permanent institutions, so their "corpus" (principal) must be maintained and it cannot be completely spent out. Second, because they have what investment types call an "infinite time horizon," they can take considerable risk, knowing they will exist long enough to recover from bad markets.

Retirees' challenges are both harder and easier. Their money does not need to last forever; they can "spend corpus," as a foundation executive would put it. But they do not know just how long it needs to last. While we all would hope to live many more years than we expect, making sure your money's lifespan is at least as long as yours is a challenge. Investment geeks call this "longevity risk."

Bengen found in his research that a retiree who spent (withdrew from investment accounts) no more than 4% of her assets each year, raising the amount each year for inflation, could expect her portfolio to last roughly 30 years, in virtually all past market conditions. So if she started at age 65, her assets would not be exhausted until age 95, or more than 10 years beyond the median life expectancy.

The logic behind the 4% rule is simple. Although you invested mainly for growth when you were working, in retirement you will not be able to replace market losses from earned income, so you will need to reallocate your portfolio towards less risky assets. (This will be discussed further in Chapter 2.) Bengen used a 50/50 stocks/bonds portfolio in his back testing. If the long-run average return on stocks is about 9% and bonds about 4%, then the portfolio's average return would be 6.5%. Subtract 2.5% average inflation nets a 4% real (i.e., inflation-adjusted) return. (Note that these are rough long-term historical averages and subject to change. In particular, we believe that average returns will be lower in the new normal.)

Another way to think about this is that for a given sum to last an assumed 30 years of your remaining life (e.g., from ages 65 to 95), only 3.3% of it could be withdrawn per year, assuming no growth in the remaining (not-withdrawn) assets. This illustrates the principle that lower investment returns mandate a lower withdrawal rate. Inflation will increase the withdrawals necessary to maintain constant purchasing power, while investment returns will extend the life of the remaining assets. Withdrawal rates in the 3% to 4% range seem reasonable.

But 4% May Be Too Much!

The 4% rule of thumb depends on many assumptions, all unknowable, including investment rates of return, inflation rates, and lifespans.

At the time of writing, bond rates of return are at historic lows because central banks throughout the world are suppressing interest rates, sometimes termed "the war on savers." And much of the money expansion that central banks have engineered have propelled stock returns higher. Historically, abnormally high stock gains have been followed by very low gains, and sometimes sharp losses. Also, undeniable trends like slowing population growth throughout advanced economies—the "new normal" we introduce in Chapter 5—will lower asset returns compared to earlier times when demographics were more favorable , such as when the baby boomers first entered the workforce. So returns over the next few years are unlikely to reach long-term average returns mentioned above. Lower returns require lower withdrawal rates.

In addition, the inflation rate faced by seniors is often higher than the headline rate for typical urban consumers. This is mainly because seniors spend a larger share of their budget on services, where prices typically rise faster than on goods. (It is hard to improve productivity of many services, but most manufactured goods are today made far more cheaply than a few generations ago.) Many services must be performed locally, with developed world pay scales. But most goods can be produced elsewhere at lower wages, then shipped to the developed world. Over the past few decades the inflation rate for seniors has been about one-fifth higher than the headline rate. So if the headline rate is 5%, seniors might face 6% inflation. While 1% seems trivial, it compounds over a 30+-year retirement.

Finally, there is no sign that lengthening lifespans will reverse. Quite the opposite: diseases that just a few decades ago caused premature death are being medically managed, or cured entirely. The most fearsome diseases in the minds of older people aren't physical but neurological, such as dementia and Alzheimer's. Such ailments were less prevalent in the past because few people lived long enough for them to manifest.

For all these reasons, a lower withdrawal rate than 4% is prudent. It will take considerable research to update Bengen's work for 21st century realities. For the present, we will assume a target withdrawal rate of 2.5% of assets, with the amount increasing each year to reflect price inflation. This may ultimately be found too conservative, but it is better for your money's lifespan to exceed your own than the opposite. (In later chapters we will occasionally use a 3% rate to make the math easier to follow.)

Your "Number"

Choose your target income in retirement. Conventional wisdom says that your "replacement ratio"—the fraction of your pre-retirement income you need to maintain a similar lifestyle—is perhaps 80% or 85%, although some argue as low as 70% if you have very simple tastes. But if you have deferred aspirations of expensive passions like travel, your replacement ratio might be 115% to 125% of your pre-retirement income. Cruises and first-class travel aren't cheap.

Once you know that target income, you can subtract from it any pension or similar income you expect to receive, such as Social Security or annuity income. The remainder is what must come from your assets, that is, the amount you need to withdraw. Here is an example.

Pre-retirement income:	$60,000
Desired replacement ratio:	× 120%
Target retirement income:	= **$72,000**
Minus: Social Security income	− $26,000
Minus: Pension-like income	− $ 6,000
Withdrawals from assets:	= **$40,000**

Required assets at start of retirement:
$40,000/2.5% = $40,000 × 40 = **$1.6 million**

In this example, Social Security and pension-like income such as annuities are expected to provide almost half ($32,000 or 44%) of the total income needed. But the other $40,000 (56%) that must come from assets implies a necessary portfolio of $1.6 million.

Your own circumstances will be different: You may have more, or less, pension-like income; you may wish to replace more, or less, than 120% of your pre-retirement income; or you may have reason to expect to live an unusually long or short remaining life. But the basic math is as shown here. Table 1-1 on page 10–11 shows target retirement asset levels for many illustrative situations.

Two cells in the table are in bold, representing the range of plausible options for a typical household with $60,000 in working income and fairly modest retirement aspirations (a 90% replacement ratio). These represent a rough minimum for anyone who wishes a middle-class lifestyle in retirement. The left bolded cell shows assets needed under a very high withdrawal rate of 5%: $1.08 million in assets. The right bolded cell requires twice the assets ($2.16 million) because only half the rate of withdrawal (2.5%) is planned. Higher income aspirations shown lower in the table imply higher asset targets, as a mathematical truism.

Table 1-1 Assets Needed to Support Retirement Spending After (Net of) Pension-like Income

Pre-retirement Income	Repl Ratio	Target Retirement Spending from Assets	Shorter Lifespan, High Returns		
			5.0%	4.5%	4.0%
$60,000	80%	$48,000	$960,000	$1,066,667	$1,200,000
	90%	$54,000	**$1,080,000**	$1,200,000	$1,350,000
	100%	$60,000	$1,200,000	$1,333,333	$1,500,000
	110%	$66,000	$1,320,000	$1,466,667	$1,650,000
	120%	$72,000	$1,440,000	$1,600,000	$1,800,000
$80,000	80%	$64,000	$1,280,000	$1,422,222	$1,600,000
	90%	$72,000	$1,440,000	$1,600,000	$1,800,000
	100%	$80,000	$1,600,000	$1,777,778	$2,000,000
	110%	$88,000	$1,760,000	$1,955,556	$2,200,000
	120%	$96,000	$1,920,000	$2,133,333	$2,400,000
$100,000	80%	$80,000	$1,600,000	$1,777,778	$2,000,000
	90%	$90,000	$1,800,000	$2,000,000	$2,250,000
	100%	$100,000	$2,000,000	$2,222,222	$2,500,000
	110%	$110,000	$2,200,000	$2,444,444	$2,750,000
	120%	$120,000	$2,400,000	$2,666,667	$3,000,000
$150,000	80%	$120,000	$2,400,000	$2,666,667	$3,000,000
	90%	$135,000	$2,700,000	$3,000,000	$3,375,000
	100%	$150,000	$3,000,000	$3,333,333	$3,750,000
	110%	$165,000	$3,300,000	$3,666,667	$4,125,000
	120%	$180,000	$3,600,000	$4,000,000	$4,500,000
$200,000	80%	$160,000	$3,200,000	$3,555,556	$4,000,000
	90%	$180,000	$3,600,000	$4,000,000	$4,500,000
	100%	$200,000	$4,000,000	$4,444,444	$5,000,000
	110%	$220,000	$4,400,000	$4,888,889	$5,500,000
	120%	$240,000	$4,800,000	$5,333,333	$6,000,000

Note: These computations are based on income needed from assets—i.e., net of any pension-like income such as Social Security or annuities, or income earned in part-time work.

Longer Lifespan, Low Returns		
3.5%	**3.0%**	**2.5%**
$1,371,429	$1,600,000	$1,920,000
$1,542,857	$1,800,000	**$2,160,000**
$1,714,286	$2,000,000	$2,400,000
$1,885,714	$2,200,000	$2,640,000
$2,057,143	$2,400,000	$2,880,000
$1,828,571	$2,133,333	$2,560,000
$2,057,143	$2,400,000	$2,880,000
$2,285,714	$2,666,667	$3,200,000
$2,514,286	$2,933,333	$3,520,000
$2,742,857	$3,200,000	$3,840,000
$2,285,714	$2,666,667	$3,200,000
$2,571,429	$3,000,000	$3,600,000
$2,857,143	$3,333,333	$4,000,000
$3,142,857	$3,666,667	$4,400,000
$3,428,571	$4,000,000	$4,800,000
$3,428,571	$4,000,000	$4,800,000
$3,857,143	$4,500,000	$5,400,000
$4,285,714	$5,000,000	$6,000,000
$4,714,286	$5,500,000	$6,600,000
$5,142,857	$6,000,000	$7,200,000
$4,571,429	$5,333,333	$6,400,000
$5,142,857	$6,000,000	$7,200,000
$5,714,286	$6,666,667	$8,000,000
$6,285,714	$7,333,333	$8,800,000
$6,857,143	$8,000,000	$9,600,000

What the table makes clear is: Unless you expect a very generous pension, maintaining something close to your spending level when you were working will require *several million dollars* in assets. Your target "number" is in the seven figures. This makes the statistics about actual household savings mentioned earlier absolutely chilling.

So $10,000 in savings may allow for perhaps $250 *a year* in spending—less than a middle-class family spends in *two days*. Clearly, large swathes of American households are not ready for retirement. This will have profound implications for our economy, society, and public finances. For example, it isn't hard to foresee senior citizens who have not saved (and who vote at high rates) voting for new taxes on young workers (who vote much less frequently) to pay for public retirement programs.

This book is not for the many ostriches who failed to prepare and now desperately hope to make up for lost time. There are many books on getting out of debt and developing a habit of saving. Chapter 25 should discourage you from some of the most common mistakes investors make when they try to dig out of their holes.

But this book is directed to smart investors like you. You followed the advice of financial pundits, who urged you to:

- ▶ Save a large portion of your salary—10% to 15%.
- ▶ Make use of tax-advantaged programs like 401(k)s and IRAs.
- ▶ Contribute at least as much as your employer matches, if you are fortunate enough to have a match available.
- ▶ Invest your savings in a diverse portfolio, using mutual funds (and now ETFs); rely significantly on index funds to minimize your investment expenses.
- ▶ Weight your portfolio heavily in stocks early in life, and rebalance into bonds as retirement approaches.

All of this advice was supported by reams of research. Some of it won the Nobel Prize. But it was a product of its time—the particular conditions of the late 20th century. Since the 2008-09 recession, we are operating in a "new normal" and we need a new map.

Some of the new truths about retirement planning include:

1. **Higher taxes and inflation are in our future.** The "new normal" that has followed the 2008–09 recession (outlined in Chapter 4) is being driven by unstoppable demographic forces. Shrinking populations will not be able to pay for existing generous government programs at current tax rates. Developed world governments will raise taxes very significantly, probably by a factor of 100% to 200%. When that fails, they will print more money, leading to higher inflation. Dust off your leisure suit: the '70s are coming back! Inflation will hit retirees especially hard: because the things they buy (like health care) typically rise in price the fastest, and because their fixed incomes cannot compensate for inflation. This book will comment on the classic inflation hedges such as real estate, precious metals, and other commodities, and show you their place in your portfolio.

2. **It's the *income*, stupid.** Throughout the several decades in which you accumulated assets, you invested primarily for growth. But growth investments like stocks are volatile, and volatility is something you will tolerate much less once you are solely dependent on those assets for living expenses. Retirees have typically met income needs with CDs, bonds, and annuities; but historically low interest rates make these poor income sources, especially under inflation. This book will introduce "alternative" investments that can help.

3. You structured your portfolio to accumulate smoothly. You will need to put as much care planning for **decumulation**. Once you no longer have a steady paycheck, you need to arrange your assets to provide you income with equal stability. Tips to do this are a major theme of this book.

One of the authors' last retirement books, *Your Macroeconomic Edge: Investing Strategies in the Post-Recession World* (*YME*), explained the new normal at length, with a few chapters applying its lessons for retirement planners. The world predicted in *YME* has now arrived. *It's the Income, Stupid!* expands on *YME* with practical advice for smart investors. Simply by being smart in your planning, you are already ahead of 80% of Americans. With your new knowledge of the secrets contained in this book, you will join the handful who can be stress-free.

CHAPTER 2

The Lopsided Mountain of Retirement Planning

You may be age 70 and retired, age 60 and preparing for retirement, or age 40 and a long-range planner. Regardless, it is important to understand the stages of your financial life.

You will experience a total of four phases:

▶ **Stage I** was *dependence*: you relied for your care on parents. You had no money concerns because you had no money; your basic needs were paid for, and you spent little beyond those. Typically this stage lasts from roughly birth to 25.

▶ **Stage II** was *independence and short-term accumulation*: When you left your parents' home, it was with a job that allowed you control over your economic life. You had to learn how to keep your expenses below your income. In time, you learned to save to achieve short-term aspirations: a car, a vacation, a house downpayment, kids, maybe further education. This stage typically occupies ages 25 to 45.

▶ **Stage III** is *wealth accumulation*: You realize that you will not work forever, so you increase your savings to accumulate assets so that you can spend them down once you no longer work. If you've learned about investments (or hired an advisor), you invested those savings—probably in stocks or stock mutual funds—so that they grow in value until you need them decades hence. This stage runs from ages 45 to between 60 and 70, although really smart investors (like you!) began accumulating even earlier.

▶ **Stage IV** is *decumulation* (also known as "distribution" or "retirement spending"): You will derive all or most of your income from your accumulated assets. Those assets need to be redeployed from the *growth* focus that was appropriate in your accumulation phase, to an *income* focus. You also will find that you can no longer tolerate volatility as you could when your need for available money was still decades away. You can no longer afford to wait for your portfolio to bounce back after a market crash. Even normal swings—which are becoming more pronounced—will be unsettling when you can't backfill them with earned income. Where you spend your money will change over this phase. In the early years it may be on discretionary items like travel, toys, or gifts for the grandkids. In later years your spending will skew towards health care. As time passes, you will rely increasingly on assured income to meet your (escalating) fixed costs and less on choosing what to sell to meet discretionary expenses. As we are all living longer, it is entirely possible that your stage IV may be longer than stage III. In fact, it is prudent to financially plan for that, so you do not outlive your assets.

Your assets in the last two phases are like a lopsided mountain—a slow climb up in ages 40 through 70, and then (hopefully) an even slower descent.

This book will concentrate on the decumulation phase. But since knowing your destination helps plan your journey, one of the last chapters will also address readers who may have decades before they retire. You can use those decades well. This chapter emphasizes stages III (accumulation) and IV (decumulation).

Stage III, Long-Term Accumulation: Be the Ant, Not the Grasshopper

You are familiar with the conventional wisdom about how to accumulate enough assets to retire:

▶ Save a considerable share (10% to 15%) of your earnings. Common rules of thumb are you should accumulate 2x salary by age 40, 5x by age 55, 10x by age 60, and 15x by your late 60s, if you plan to replace 100% of your working income from your assets. (Even this may not be enough. The goal of 15x your salary by retirement implies planning for a 6.7% withdrawal rate, which is foolhardy unless you are sure your portfolio will grow quickly in retirement, or you won't live long.) The exact multiples depend on your target income, since Social Security will be a smaller share of a larger income. Your multiple may be modestly lower if your target income is fairly low, and moderately higher if the opposite. Make the most use of the power of compounding by investing as early as possible.

▶ Minimize taxes by taking the most advantage of tax-preferred accounts like 401(k)s and IRAs. At least contribute the maximum amount your employer matches (often 3% to 6% of salary, where it still exists).

▶ Invest in diversified, low-cost mutual funds and ETFs. Buy and hold—do not time the market.

▶ Weight your portfolio heavily with stocks when young, because your retirement will still be decades away and you can patiently ride out bear markets. As retirement approaches, gradually change your asset allocation to favor bonds, which are much less volatile than stocks. A common rule of thumb is: bonds' proportion of your portfolio in percent should equal your age. So a 70-year old retiree should have only 30% of her portfolio in stocks and stock funds.

This wasn't your grandparents' retirement planning. Many of them could expect a modest but steady pension. On the other hand, they might live only five or 10 years—not 30—after they stopped working. Smart investors like you have navigated unfamiliar territory with little help from native guides. It required superior *discipline*: to spend much less than you earned; to *invest*, not speculate; and to manage a *portfolio*, as opposed to a series of unrelated investments. Congratulate yourself, and your patient family.

Now, the bad news: While the broad skills you gained through decades of discipline will still be useful, many of these specifics will be downright counterproductive. Many excellent accumulators make lousy decumulators. ("If I buy a new car now, I will give up an extra $100,000 in 10 years.") But the whole point of all that accumulation was to eventually spend it—either on your own consumption, or on bequests to family members or to charities.

The problem is that you need a plan that is as thoughtful about generating funds to meet your spending needs in retirement as your accumulation plan was while you were working. In other words, how can you organize your assets to generate a regular paycheck in retirement?

Stage IV, Decumulation (Distribution): It's the *Income*, Stupid

Traditional income planning meant one thing: fixed income investments like bonds and CDs. If long-term bonds were paying 5% or 6%, they exceeded the 4% guideline, so you could comfortably spend coupon payments without touching the principal. If you did not need to sell the bonds to produce income, you took no interest rate risk because you held the bond until maturity. In the early 20th century, bond "ladders" were a common strategy: buy several bonds of staggered maturity dates—such as 5, 10, 15, and 20 years in the future—and hold each until they mature. Choose those maturities around a "chunky" cash need, such as a kid's college tuition or a major purchase (such as a long-planned dream vacation, or paying off your mortgage). When a bond matures, spend the principal if you have planned for it; otherwise, purchase another bond with a maturity that extends beyond your latest-maturing bond. (In this example, you could invest in a 25-year bond that matures five years after your latest-maturing bond.) It's a simple but durable system, used by wealthy families and institutions for hundreds of years. And it is quite stable, since income is fixed and interest rate risk has been eliminated. Bond ladders are often the premise for many financial plans that shift portfolio weights out of stocks and into bonds as retirement approaches. But they have become less common as bond returns have fallen over the past generation.

There are two problems with this conventional approach, which are mirror images: Inflation and interest rate suppression. Inflation undermined it in the 1970s, and financial repression undermines it today.

Inflation is deadly to bond prices. Interest rates must rise to compensate for rising prices, to assure interest payments maintain the same constant purchasing power. But fixed income bonds, the usual type, have just that: *fixed* income. Traditional bonds' coupons do not rise when prices do. So a bond paying 5% when inflation is at 2% offers a "real" (inflation-adjusted) interest rate of 3%. But if inflation rises to 6%, the coupon does not change: it is fixed at 5%. Now the real interest rate is -1%. Lenders are paying borrowers to rent their money. This is not what an investor hopes for.

Inflation is usually a handmaiden to an overheated economy. After the inflation of the late 20th century, the U.S. Treasury began issuing TIPS bonds (Treasury Inflation Protected Securities) with a variable interest rate indexed to the consumer price index, which in theory eliminates inflation risk.

Because traditional bond *coupons* do not change, all new developments are instead reflected in bond *prices*. In the example above, a 5% coupon means that the bondholder receives $50 per year on a bond whose face value is $1,000. If interest rates rise to 10%, the $50 coupon doesn't change. Instead the bond's price drops to $500, because $50 is 10% of $500. Ouch. Fortunately, this only matters if you wish to sell the bond before maturity. Its price will converge on $1,000 as maturity nears. So if you hold it to maturity you can be sure to get $1,000 back from the bond issuers, as long as they do not default. But $1,000 may buy a lot less by then.

But the other problem occurs when economies are soft: deflation. Central banks try to preempt deflation with massive monetary stimulus: that is, they expand the money supply to lower interest rates to encourage more borrowing and spending. This "financial repression" can create a "war on savers," with extremely low interest rates—too low to offer the returns assumed in the 4% withdrawal rule.

So a pure bond strategy is a recipe for disappointment at least (under deflation and financial repression), or disaster (under inflation). That's why advisors have traditionally suggested keeping some of your portfolio (conventionally, 100% minus your age) in stocks, which are a better inflation hedge. Companies can raise their prices when their costs rise; bonds cannot. Holding bonds to maturity, and buying inflation-indexed bonds like TIPS, can also help. But no bond strategy can overcome repressed interest rates. We discuss this trajectory of asset allocations, called the "glide path," and its inverse in Chapter 3.

Income Without Bonds

Bonds aren't the only income-producing investment. Here are some others. These are discussed in more detail in later chapters.

- ▶ **Dividend stocks.** Originally, most common stocks paid a dividend: a quarterly cash payment to shareholders paid from profits, set by the company board of directors. In fact, one of the rigorous methods used to value common stocks was called the "dividend discount model." The long-term dividend yield of a major stock index like the S&P 500 is currently about 2%— average annual dividend payments divided by a stock's price is about .02. Companies are categorized by the fraction of their profits paid out in dividends, known as the payout ratio. Growth companies don't pay dividends at all (a payout ratio of 0%); their boards feel that retaining profits to fuel faster growth is the better option. Many tech companies spurn dividends. Apple only began paying a dividend in the late 2000s. In contrast, mature companies with limited growth prospects may pay the majority of their profits in dividends. Utilities are the classic example: they can expect little growth in demand if their service territory is mature, so they do not need to retain much profit to accommodate customer growth.

▶ **Preferred stock.** Besides common stock, many corporations issue "preferred" stock, so-called because in liquidation its shareholders are in a preferred position ahead of common stock-holders: they get paid ahead of common shareholders out of any liquidation proceeds. But all stockholders are behind bond-holders. Preferred shares are equity/fixed income hybrids: they pay a coupon like a bond, but their price varies with the fortunes of the company. This is most true for "convertible preferreds," where the shareholder has the option of converting his preferred stock into common stock. This will be attractive if common shares rise above the conversion price. So these hybrids typically are more volatile than common stock, but less than bonds.

▶ **Alternative investments.** This is a catchall term for a wide range of investments that generally are also hybrids: they typically pay a dividend or coupon, but can rise when the issuer's business results improve. Some examples include:

- **REITs:** Real estate investment trusts are like mutual funds that own income-producing property. Income comes from rents paid by their tenants. REITs differ based on the type of property they own (residences, offices, stores, hospitals, industrial plants, etc.) and by other characteristics.

- **MLPs:** Similar to REITs, Master Limited Partnerships typically own energy properties. They may be "upstream," such as producing oil or gas wells, "midstream" pipelines, or "downstream," such as refineries.
- **BDCs:** Business Development Companies lend to private firms such as small and midsized businesses, usually at floating rates of interest.

All of these are organized as what tax professionals term "pass through entities" in which nearly all profits must be passed through to the owners. If at least 90% of profits are distributed, these entities pay no corporate tax. So dividend payments are high, often two to four times the yield of common stock. But because few profits are retained, these firms cannot grow quickly. Alternatives make great sense for income, but less so for capital gains.

"Alternatives" is a broad catchall designation for anything that isn't a stock or a bond. It can include classes of assets like REITs, MLPs, and BDCs, as well as alternative investment strategies that move among stocks and bonds in novel ways.

Each of these investments also helps counter one of the greatest scourges of retirees: inflation. REITs and MLPs own real property that typically performs well under inflationary conditions. And because BDCs' loans are usually at floating rates, the BDC's income will rise when interest rates do, such as when inflation accelerates. Some BDCs also make equity investments in their borrowers, allowing for some potential upside and inflation protection.

Alternative investments are an important secret to a stress-free retirement, so they will get considerable attention in this book. Chapters 10 through 22 will discuss these and other alternatives in more detail.

Alternatives also have another important advantage: lower volatility than common stocks. You will wish to lower your portfolio's volatility as you move from accumulation to decumulation. Understanding the correlation of each investment with common stocks—how much they move in tandem, vs. in opposite directions—is another secret essential to de-stressing your retirement. It will be explained in Chapter 3.

There exist both public and private versions of each of these alternatives—termed "traded" and "nontraded." Their respective advantages and disadvantages will be explored later. Nontraded versions have some surprising advantages related to volatility and correlations as described in Chapter 16.

The remainder of this book explains how to gradually convert your portfolio from growth-oriented to income-oriented for the realities of the new normal. But first, a review of the smart steps you took as you accumulated.

CHAPTER 3

The Accumulation Phase
. . . .
Conventional and Unconventional Wisdom

Smart investors know that they should not buy everything that Wall Street sells. If you have accumulated a reasonably large nest egg—at least several hundred thousand dollars—that puts you in the top few percent of American savers; you have educated yourself in the conventional wisdom about investing. These inherited verities stem from voluminous financial research. An incomplete list of these truths include the following.

Compounding Works Best When It Persists the Longest

Therefore, start investing early and continuously. When Albert Einstein was asked what the most powerful force in the universe was, he said, "Compound interest." Letting gains on an investment compound can turn a linear growth process into an exponential one.

You have probably seen illustrations that compare two twins, Sally Spendthrift and Franny Frugal (or equally silly names). Sally parties throughout her 20s and does not begin saving for retirement until age 30. Franny begins saving at a young age (21), does so for 10 years, then stops. So Sally saves a constant amount for 35 years (from 30 through 65), while Franny saves the same annual amount for only 10 years (21 through 30). Yet Franny ends up with a much larger nest egg than Sally! This is not due to superior investing skill: the twins are assumed to earn the same annual rate of return. It is due to *time*. Franny's 10-year head start more than compensated for the fact that she stopped saving decades before Sally could. Take a spreadsheet and check it out for yourself. Every young person should. Most middle-aged persons will be dismayed, but not smart investors like you.

You can think of the value of any investment as having two components:

1. the principal you saved, which required work and sacrifice;
2. the gains earned passively, which required only time and patience.

Because Franny started earlier, a far larger share of her nest egg came the easy way (passively), rather than from work.

For plausible rates of return, an investment that you hold for five years may be two-thirds principal and one-third gain. But hold it for 30 years and it might be one-tenth principal and nine-tenths gain.

Stocks Have the Highest Long-Term Returns

During accumulation stage, keep the bulk of your portfolio in stocks.
Long-term average returns for stocks have been close to 9% to 10% per year (perhaps 7% real—net of inflation—return), while bonds have returned about 4% to 5% (about 2% real). At those rates a stock investment will double in about seven years, while a bond investment will need just under 15 years—about twice as long.

To take the best advantage of the power of compounding, invest mostly in stocks, and reinvest any dividends. While stocks are far more volatile than bonds, they have never lost money over a 20-year holding period, and only very rarely over 10 years. (This reflects nearly a century of history, but may not apply in the future.) So when the time when you will need to sell is still far in the future you can weight your portfolio heavily in stocks or stock funds. You will have ample time to wait for a market rebound. This is the premise behind the traditional idea that stocks' share of your portfolio in percent should equal 100 minus your age. As time passes and the date when you need the money approaches, you should gradually reduce your allocation to volatile assets like stocks and raise the allocation to less volatile ones—traditionally bonds, but this book will also make a case for alternatives.

Glide Paths and Updrafts

The trajectory just described is the conventional wisdom. It calls for your asset allocation to be very heavily weighted toward stocks early in your accumulation phase, gradually shifting from stocks to fixed income as you age and your decumulation phase approaches. This is known as the "glide path," in which your stock portfolio slowly descends to earth over time as you sell shares to buy bonds. It makes intuitive sense because volatility becomes less tolerable when you have less time for your portfolio to bounce back from a market downturn. But this canon has been revised significantly over the past two decades.

First, inflation must be hedged against. A fixed income portfolio in retirement (e.g., a bond ladder) may have been adequate when the purchasing power of its coupon payments remained stable—i.e., there was little inflation. The 1970s offered a very rude awakening to retirees whose income was entirely fixed: it was fixed in nominal dollars, but shrinking in purchasing power. This led to the 100 minus your age guideline: until you reached age 100 (and had well exceeded normal life expectancy), some of your assets would remain in stocks to hedge against inflation.

Second, recent research by Rob Arnott and his colleagues at Research Affiliates, as well as Wade Pfau of the American College of Retirement and his frequent coauthor Michael Kitces, suggests reversing the glide path in late retirement. This is known as the "inverse glide path." The math of this is irrefutable: stocks' returns are so superior to bonds' that your portfolio's life will be maximized by keeping a sizable fraction of it in equities throughout—and *increasing* late in retirement to extend its life. But this is only possible if you can accept stocks' volatility in retirement as equably as you could when still working. This requires organizing your portfolio so that you do not need to spend the volatile parts imminently. That is the core purpose of this book, encapsulated in Chapter 6.

Averages Can Mislead You!

As you have accumulated assets, chances are that you have paid some general attention to your portfolio's average returns. For example, if you want your portfolio to double in value by the time you plan to retire in 15 years, your goal would be about a 5% average annual return. (This is because 1.05^{15} = just over 2.) Focusing on the average return recognizes that annual returns can vary widely, but their cumulative effect will be a compounded average.

But this perspective can be misleading, in two important ways. One is prosaic but straightforward, and the other is more profound.

Arithmetic vs. Geometric Averages

Consider the annual returns for the hypothetical $10,000 investment below:

Year	Annual Return	Balance
0	—	$10,000
1	+10%	$11,000
2	+10%	$12,100
3	0%	$12,100
4	−10%	$10,890
5	−10%	$9,801

−1.99% Cumulative Return
0% Average Return (arithmetic)
−0.4% Average Annualized Return
(IRR or Internal Rate of Return)

The asset enjoyed two good years, a flat year, then two down years. Average annual returns were zero. But its value did not end at the same place where it started. That is because the returns *in absolute dollars* differed each year. Because the asset first grew in value, its later losses were from a higher base, so were larger in absolute dollars. This is why experienced investors hate to lose money. They know that a 50% decline requires a subsequent 100% recovery to get back to even.

Investments that quote annual average returns ignore this. If the asset grows in value on average, down years will have a disproportionate effect on returns that this *arithmetic* average does not capture. Since you care most about the asset's cumulative value when you will sell it, the *geometric* average return is much more relevant. Geometric returns recognize that growth is a compounding process, so they combine years through multiplication, not addition.

The better average is a *compound annual growth rate* (CAGR), which is a geometric computation that reflects compounding. This is an increasingly common statistic, but still not universally used. You should insist on seeing, or calculating, this CAGR to compare investments in common terms. CAGR is simply:

CAGR = [(Ending value) / (Starting value)] $\wedge$ (1/# of years) −1

So if the stock's current price is $200 vs. a price of $100 when you bought it five years ago, its CAGR is:

[$200 / $100] $\wedge$ (1/5) − 1 = 2 $\wedge$ 0.2 −1 = 1.149 − 1 = **14.9%**

…because $100 growing at 14.9% annually will compound to $200 in five years.

This is a better reflection of the asset's return over long periods of time. But remember that any average return omits volatility. Modern portfolio theory, discussed later in this chapter, captures both return *and* risk.

The bottom line: Ignore arithmetic average returns. Accept only geometric averages. Fortunately, the CAGR metric is increasingly common. But when it is not cited you can still compute it easily. Don't forget that it is only an *average* return and does not capture volatility.

Sequence of Returns Risk

When you are accumulating assets and leaving them in place to enjoy the benefits of compounding, you can be indifferent about the sequence over which you earn positive returns. A 50% return followed by a 1% return will compound to the same result—about 51% cumulative returns—regardless of the order in which you experienced those returns. But as the previous section illustrated, you will be anything but indifferent about negative returns. A simple example will illustrate. Assume that your portfolio begins at a value of $100 and experiences one year of -50% returns and two years of +50% returns.

Loss earlier		*Loss later*		
Starting value	$100	$100		
After 1st year	$50	(−50% return)	$150	(+50% return)
After 2nd year	$75	(+50% return)	$225	(+50% return)
After 3rd year	$102.50	(+50% return)	$112.50	(−50% return)

In the first scenario, your cumulative growth is 2.5%—less than 1% per year. In the second scenario you earned 12.5% cumulatively, more than 4% per year. *When negative years are included, the sequence of returns matters.*

You cannot control or predict investment returns, but a large part of your negative "returns" are predictable: they are called withdrawals. You might be thinking that you cannot control your returns (and you would be right), but you can control the timing of when

Figure 3-1 Sequence of Returns Comparison

	YEAR	Portfolio 1 Return	Portfolio 1 Balance* $100,000	Portfolio 2 Return	Portfolio 2 Balance* $100,000
	0				
The combination of the market's impact and the $7,000 yearly withdrawal leaves Portfolio 1 with less than $76,000 at the end of year one.	1	-18.39%	$75,897	26.57%	$117,710
	2	-19.14%	$55,710	19.61%	$132,420
	3	-4.59%	$46,475	5.26%	$132,017
	4	18.47%	$46,766	16.57%	$145,733
	5	6.79%	$42,466	33.60%	$185,347
	6	14.30%	$40,537	21.23%	$216,210
	7	-15.39%	$28,376	13.92%	$238,332
	8	14.59%	$24,495	-1.61%	$227,608
	9	8.95%	$19,060	21.03%	$267,002
	10	19.52%	$14,414	16.21%	$302,148
	11	20.72%	$8,951	20.72%	$356,303
Portfolio 1 runs out of money by year 13 because of the negative returns it experiences at the outset.	12	16.21%	$2,267	19.52%	$417,486
	13	21.03%	$0	8.95%	$447,225
	14	-1.61%	$0	14.59%	$504,454
	15	13.92%	$0	-15.39%	$420,896
	16	21.23%	$0	14.30%	$473,083
	17	33.60%	$0	6.79%	$497,730
	18	16.57%	$0	18.47%	$581,367
	19	5.26%	$0	-4.59%	$548,004
	20	19.61%	$0	-19.14%	$437,456
	21	26.57%	$0	-18.39%	$351,295

*Starting balance = $100,000;
Withdrawals = $7,000/year

you begin taking withdrawals—i.e., when you stop working and begin relying on your assets for living expenses.

The example in Figure 3-1, from data by financial advisor Bob Lindquist, illuminates the sequence of returns problem dramatically. Both scenarios use historical return data for a major stock index. Scenario B shows those returns in actual sequence; scenario A merely reverses the order of that sequence. Each portfolio begins with $100,000 and has $7,000 per year withdrawn. Over the 21 years shown, each experiences five down years, with three of them serious. But those down years are clustered near the beginning of Scenario A and near the end of Scenario B.

In scenario A, the combined blows of several early down years cannot compensate for withdrawals—they magnify them. The portfolio falls quickly and is exhausted by year 12 (thereby missing the good returns in years 13 to 21). When the sequence of returns is reversed in Scenario B, strong early returns more than compensate for withdrawals: the portfolio's value grows, smartly, and does not peak until year 18. At year 21 it is still worth 3.5 times its starting value.

The obvious but impractical conclusion is that it is better to retire before a bull market ends than in a bear market. Of course, if you knew when this will occur, you would not need this book!

A more subtle and important conclusion is that you have very good reasons to be concerned about negative returns once you begin drawing on your assets for income. Investment losses will compound the effects of your drawdowns. So it becomes doubly important to smooth fluctuations.

Market Timing Is Often an Aspiration, Rarely a Reality

Market inflection (turning) points offer little warning and happen very suddenly.

In a perfect world we would anticipate turns in asset prices and buy just before an upswing and sell just before a downswing. The subtext behind a few financial advisors' value proposition is that they have superior foresight and can predict inflection points. Most know better because there are two reasons to doubt this.

First, people so clairvoyant would not be selling their services for fees and commissions; they would be keeping their gift secret, investing their own funds to get very, very rich.

Second, Eugene Fama of the University of Chicago posited that markets are efficient. In this context "efficiency" means that new information about an asset will be reflected in the asset's price very quickly. For instance, if you know that a biotech company's clinical trial just showed its new drug was not effective, you would wish to sell your stock very quickly, before the price falls. Your act will drive the price down, so its market price will quickly reflect the bad news. Markets are not efficient because of altruism, but the opposite: possessors of new information try to act quickly while it provides them an advantage over other investors. The logical extension of this principle is to computerize it so that humans do not delay action; this is high frequency trading (HFT), which now accounts for the majority of volume on major stock exchanges.

Market efficiency is well-established for very large and liquid markets like the New York Stock Exchange. While Fama's theory is formally known as the "efficient market *hypothesis*," which is held by different academics with differing intensity, it has become dogma in most university economics and finance departments.

Because of the speed with which new information affects asset prices, markets turn very quickly. Many studies have shown that over a long period (decades), simply missing a handful of the strongest "up" days significantly reduces an investor's long-term returns. Similarly, selling into a down market often keeps the investor out of subsequent upturn.

So the canonical wisdom is that investors should *not* try to time the market. Even being 90% right will cost you return. Instead, the standard advice is to *buy and hold*: Maintain exposure to an asset class through thick and thin.

Numerous studies by the research firm Dalbar have shown that the actual returns earned by index mutual fund investors are less than half of the fund's buy-and-hold returns. The difference is that an index fund does not exit the market when it drops so it doesn't miss the upturns, either. Real investors often buy *after* an asset has already risen substantially, and sell *after* it has fallen—buying high and selling low. Bad timing costs them more than half of the return they could have earned if they had stayed fully invested.

Bad timing occurs not only in selling into a bottom, but in buying at a top. Most employer retirement plans are designed instead for steady, persistent contributions by employees. When prices are high, the same contribution in dollars buys fewer units than when prices are low. Your overall price is the average of all the different prices you paid, so this approach is known as "dollar cost averaging."

Consistent, *persistent* investing, implemented as dollar cost averaging, has other advantages. It gains you immediate exposure to the asset class in which you invest, so you get the benefit of compounding. If you automate it—by deducting a consistent amount from your paycheck, for example—saving becomes relatively painless and you can accumulate far more than if savings only happens when you choose. A promising extension to this idea is "Save More Tomorrow," a brainchild of several behavioral economists. Under the program, an employee commits to saving a percentage of her paycheck each period *and* a (usually larger) percentage of any future increases. The idea is to get off the "hedonic treadmill" in which salary increases lead to spending increases without commensurate gains in happiness. Early experiments with "save more tomorrow" have been very positive.

Diversification

Diversifying softens the blow if one company runs into trouble.

Owning a given company stock exposes you to two types of risk: Individual risk that the company may experience bad news, and systemic risk that stocks in general will suffer (because of a recession, for example). Holding a diverse portfolio of a number of different companies protects against individual company risk. If one company goes bankrupt, its effect on your portfolio will only be proportional to its weight in the portfolio. Many investing advisors suggest that no individual holding should be more than 4% to 5% of your portfolio.

As a cautionary example, consider the disaster faced by Enron employees. When the company's accounting fraud was revealed and Enron declared bankruptcy in 2001, many lost more than their jobs. They had directed most or all of their 401(k) contributions into Enron stock, too. So the company's demise destroyed their future along with their present.

Advisors therefore suggest limiting the share of your retirement portfolio associated with your employer or its industry to a very small fraction, like 5% or 10%. This can be hard if they are enjoying rapid growth and your holdings are rising rapidly in value. But it is prudent, even if those gains are real (not due to fraud or crime like Enron). Fast rises are often followed by even faster falls.

Limiting any individual position in your portfolio to a small fraction like 5% means that the demise of any single company or industry will not sink your dreams. But it also means that any great success will have an equally modest impact. That is an unavoidable mathematical fact. In football terms, a prudent portfolio will see many short yardage runs, and few long balls or sacks deep in friendly territory. In baseball language: Many singles and few home runs. Smart portfolios are boring, by design.

Diversification can reduce individual company risk as each company becomes a smaller part of your portfolio. But it can never eliminate it entirely.

By the same token diversification can be overdone. Research has demonstrated that the reduction in volatility achieved by diversification has diminishing returns. That is, you reduce swings in your portfolio by lesser amounts after you have added a very few stocks to your portfolio. "Focus" investing strategies target holding only 15 or 20 stocks. Warren Buffett's Berkshire Hathaway has sometimes held more than 50% of its portfolio in four or five stocks, because he has unusual tolerance for volatility.

Volatility

A portfolio of uncorrelated assets reduces volatility.

While diversification will dampen the effect of individual risk, if all of your holdings are of the same general type (such as common stocks, or treasury bonds) it will not reduce systemic risk. An all-stock portfolio will still suffer if the entire stock market crashes.

The best way to smooth out fluctuations in your portfolio's performance is by choosing *uncorrelated* assets. This is the essential idea behind modern portfolio theory (MPT), discussed later. Here is an example.

Say your portfolio consists entirely of stock in a single oil company like Exxon Mobil (XOM). When oil prices are high its revenues will be strong, and its stock will perform well. But it will be quite volatile, rising and falling along with oil prices. You can smooth this volatility by adding another company that does well when oil prices are low, and poorly when they are high. An example would be an airline or a trucking company, whose largest expense is fuel. The two companies in your portfolio may be *negatively correlated:* their stock prices move in opposite directions when oil prices change. This greatly dampens swings in the combined portfolio.

The most integrated synthesis of conventional wisdom is modern portfolio theory. This chapter will introduce the concept briefly, and note areas of exception that will be taken up in later chapters.

Efficient Markets, Active vs. Passive Investing in the Accumulation Phase, and Financial Fragility

The most common way to diversify is through mutual funds or Exchange Traded Funds (ETFs). Decades of financial research has found that only a tiny percentage of active fund managers (who get paid to choose the specific investments they expect will outperform an unmanaged index) over long periods of time actually beat the index against which they are benchmarked. This may be because markets are efficient, so it is virtually impossible to maintain a durable edge over other investors. It certainly is affected by the significantly higher management fees charged by active managers compared to index funds—commonly four or five times higher. (Index fund expense ratios typically are about 0.2% of assets per year, while active funds often charge 1% or more.) This "fee drag" creates a major handicap that active managers rarely can overcome. Jack Bogle, founder of the Vanguard Group, which pioneered indexing, says, "In mutual funds, you get what you *don't* pay for."

Thousands of money managers sell superior performance, but only a very small percentage deliver over a long period. Smart investors like you know this and put the majority of your assets in low cost index funds during the accumulation phase. You gain exposure to the asset class and wide diversification, at very low cost. Choosing funds that are not correlated with each other can further dampen your portfolio's volatility.

Short-Term vs. Long-Term Efficiency of the Traded Markets

As just noted, the rarity of investment managers whose returns persistently exceed broad market indexes seems to be powerful evidence in favor of market efficiency. But at the same time, short-term price moves seem to contradict it. When a stock gains or loses 30% or more market value in a day without experiencing any development that would seem to justify such a radical change, it calls market efficiency into doubt. Most active fund managers premise their work on the belief that they are an individual exception to the efficient market hypothesis (EMH), or have found a niche market lacking efficiency. Finance academics have developed three versions of EMH—strong, semi-strong, and weak—to capture the range of possible levels of efficiency.

We take a simpler view. We believe that developed markets' efficiency grows over time. In the very short term, spurious events can shape prices. In the long run, reality wins out, and prices will conform to intrinsic value. In this we follow the originator of value investing, Ben Graham. He famously said, "In the short run, the market is a voting machine. In the long run, it is a weighing machine." Psychologists like Nobel prizewinner Daniel Kahneman distinguish between two systems of decision-making: System I is reflexive and intuitive, while System II is rational and deliberative. The fact that many human decisions are made using System I does not disprove the existence of System II. Likewise for market efficiency.

Our theory that efficiency grows over time pertains to the traded financial markets. Since the 2008 global financial crisis, many have challenged the EMH as it relates to the financial system as a whole. We are proponents of Hyman Minsky's *financial instability hypothesis* (FIH) which states that over time, during periods of economic expansion and rising earnings, the financial system becomes fragile, leading to economic and financial crises. As profits increase, more debt is taken on to increase profits even more. Eventually this leads to too much debt that cannot be sustained by the value of assets or by earnings. Markets overshoot. After booms there is always a bust. The smart investor needs to plan for eventual downturns and busts especially during the decumulation or income phase in retirement. During the accumulation phase, emphasizing low cost index approaches offers great opportunities to buy low during downturns.

Arguably, many markets are becoming progressively more short-term efficient as computing power becomes more prevalent (making it easier to identify assets that are underpriced or overpriced relative to the intrinsic value), and trading systems exploit these anomalies. By some estimates three-fourths of the trading volume on the New York Stock Exchange comes from high frequency trading (HFT) platforms—that is, from computer algorithms. By rapidly bidding up the price of undervalued assets, traders transmit valuation information through the market. The faster they act—and HFT strategies act in milliseconds—the more efficient they make the market. So in the long run most markets will become more and more efficient. There will be ever-less reason to pay the higher costs of active management. Investors seem to be voting with their feet, shifting hundreds of billions out of active funds into index funds in the 2010s decade.

Modern Portfolio Theory

Harry Markowitz won the Nobel Prize in economics for his development of "modern portfolio theory" (MPT). He identified the power
of a portfolio whose constituents are uncorrelated assets. Here is a
brief introduction. (We have described this in fuller [but still quite
accessible] form in Chapter 10, in our book *What Hedge Funds
Really Do* [Business Expert Press, 2014.])

We can array any asset we might include in our portfolio on a
graph of risk vs. return. Commonly, risk is measured by variation
in returns (usually defined as their standard deviation), and return
is total return—dividends plus price gains. Risk is arrayed horizon-
tally, from low to high; and return is arrayed vertically. This allows
a portfolio designer to consider the risk/return tradeoff: how much
risk must he take to raise his return? William Sharpe designed the
eponymous Sharpe ratio to capture this. The Sharpe ratio is the ratio
of return divided by risk. (More technically, it is excess return over
the risk-free rate—usually defined as the rate on short-term government securities. But that rate is essentially zero at present.)

The "best" assets in a return-per-unit-of-risk sense will appear
in the upper left part of the graph: high returns, low risk. Any assets
that are "southeast" of the upper left will be inferior in risk/return
ratio. Markowitz identified the *efficient frontier* as all assets whose
returns exceed others at the same risk level, or have higher risk for
the same return. Portfolios should combine assets on this frontier.

Visualizing this graphic, you can imagine that a portfolio
composed of, say, Asset A and Asset B should have return and risk
characteristics between those for A and B separately: closer to one
of them if it is more heavily weighted, and exactly between A and B
if they are weighted equally. ("Weight" here means the fraction of
the portfolio's total value devoted to each asset.) But here is where
correlations are critical. If A and B are uncorrelated—or even better,
negatively correlated—the combination's return will be the weighted
average of A and B, but the combined risk may be smaller than

Figure 3-2 Hypothetical Efficient Frontier: The Power of Diversification

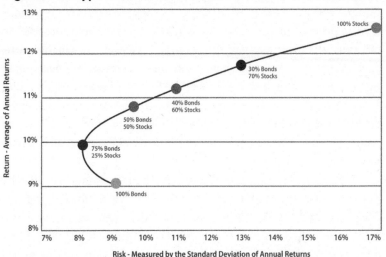

either one! If one asset zigs when the other zags, their oscillations can mutually dampen.

So constructing your overall portfolio means not only keeping each asset class within its target proportion—say, 60% stocks and 40% bonds, including regular rebalancing. It also means choosing each portfolio component with awareness of its correlation with the others', seeking to have their oscillations be out of phase so that they dampen the portfolio's swings.

In Figure 3-2, above, the return is increased when adding stocks to a bond portfolio (from 100% bonds to 25% stocks and 75% bonds), but the addition of the riskier asset class, stocks, also *decreases* risk for the overall portfolio. Thereafter, increasing stock allocations raise both return *and* risk.

Post-Modern Portfolio Theory

Critics of MPT have pointed out that investors are not equally concerned about both upward and downward deviations in returns, as MPT implies. Upward deviations are better known as positive returns and are exactly what investors seek. Downward deviations are the price of positive returns, whose frequency investors wish to minimize. They do not have symmetrical preferences. Furthermore, psychological experiments have confirmed that investors' aversion to loss is strong enough that they feel the loss of a given amount about two to two and one-half times as strongly as the same sized gain. So MPT's definition of risk as the standard deviation of returns, in which positive and negative deviations are weighted equally, misses the mark.

Post-modern portfolio theory (PMPT) accounts for this by defining risk solely in terms of downward deviations in returns (negative returns). Portfolios "optimally" designed (that is, to maximize return for a given level of risk; or to minimize risk to achieve a target rate of return) use a risk measure based only on downward deviations, i.e., downside risk. The approach in Chapter 6, which is the core idea in this book, is a natural extension of PMPT.

Unconventional Wisdom

The above truisms served you well in the late 20th century. But a new century has revealed a new normal, which calls much of the conventional wisdom into question. This is discussed in the next chapter.

CHAPTER 4

The New Normal

Readers now near the end of their accumulation phase or early in decumulation had their formative investing experiences in the late 20th century. Their experience reflected the conventional wisdom summarized in Chapter 3, driven by that era's "perfect storm" of favorable demographics and economic trends. But the 2008–09 recession and the subsequent lackluster recovery revealed starkly different conditions that cast doubt on many of these premises. This chapter summarizes the "new normal" of the investing reality, including some changes that we hadn't accurately predicted. Three inescapable trends are driving investments in the developed world.

Debt

Governments throughout the world have spent more than the tax revenues they collect, accumulating debt that has risen to levels well above their countries' GDPs. (The ratio of government debt to national GDP is a common indicator of debt burden.) When debt levels approach unaffordability, lenders shut their wallets: they stop lending. Governments then must throw spending and taxation into sudden reverse, which often can stifle a recovery or bring on a depression. Greece is only the most recent example. If the government can print the national currency (a privilege lost to countries like Greece when they joined the Euro zone), it can expand the supply of money to devalue its purchasing power, making the debt less expensive in real terms. But this comes at the cost of accelerating inflation, which can stifle investment and growth. Research by Professors Carmen Reinhart and Kenneth Rogoff suggests that the effective limit on government debt to avoid these malignant economic side effects is about 90% of GDP. Every advanced nation's debt is far above this level; Greece isn't even the worst.

When lenders go on strike, governments will first respond with spending cuts and higher tax rates (or taxing things that had never been taxed). Taxpayers will shelter income by doing less of the activity being taxed, moving funds offshore to lower-tax jurisdictions, or searching for loopholes. When revenue raised falls short of projections, governments are likely to turn to monetizing the debt by expanding the money supply, which will in time bring on higher inflation.

The combination of these acts will be stagflation: slow growth coupled with high inflation. This last occurred in the U.S. in the late 1970s. Stagflation is typically bad for stocks, as it was then.

The greatest departure from our forecast has been regarding inflation. Developed world central banks have created nearly $10 trillion in new money since 2008, and inflation has not exploded—in fact, many countries have barely avoided endemic deflation. So far it appears that the stagnating forces of debt have overwhelmed the forces of monetization/inflation.

Demographics

As societies prosper, birthrates drop. Urbanization brings households off the farm, where large families are an economic asset, into cities where they are a liability. Economic opportunities for women cause many to defer motherhood. A long-term measure of this trend is the "total fertility ratio" (TFR)—the average number of children born per woman during her lifetime. Population levels are stable at TFRs near 2.0, perhaps 2.05 to compensate for infant mortality. The rich world's TFRs fell below 2 a few decades after World War II (in Europe first, then Japan). It would be below 2 in the U.S. today but for immigration from highly fecund societies. When fewer babies are born to replace deaths, populations age and eventually shrink. There are fewer kids in schools, then fewer workers in jobs.

Younger populations must work and save to prepare for eventual retirement, while older populations mostly spend accumulated assets. Aging has a profound effect on economies, and on the prosperity of different industries. A young population will have vibrant education and construction sectors, while the strongest sectors among an older population will be health care and funeral homes.

If societies have put in place entitlement programs like retirement pensions (such as Social Security in the U.S.), those costs will rise as the number of older residents grows. Further, they will become less affordable if the number of workers who fund the entitlement system shrinks. In addition, societies, like individuals, take fewer risks and innovate less as they age. An aging population means a less dynamic economy: less invention and more resources used to support dependent populations.

Many things can change between the time of an economic forecast and its realization that often render such forecasts downright embarrassing. But a demographic forecast is surer. The number of births today provides an excellent estimate of the number of 25-year-olds a generation from now. Similarly, the number of 40-year-olds today is a solid predictor of the number of 65-year-olds 25 years hence.

A slowing birthrate has undoubtedly been an environmental boon, since slackening population growth exerts decelerating stress on the biosphere. But its handmaiden, an aging society, is not an unmixed blessing. The advanced economies felt the demographic slowdown first: Japan most severely, followed by Western Europe. America's demographic slowdown has been muted by immigration. But for many developing countries entering the global middle class, their birthrates are also falling rapidly, and their societies are aging. Birthrates in poor vs. prosperous provinces in China (inland vs. coastal) and India (northern vs. southern) vary by a factor of three to six, with the more prosperous provinces already below replacement rates. As long as their economies continue to improve, their birthrates will decline and their populations will age. This is most visible in China, because of its longstanding "one child" policy (recently relaxed slightly): China's median age will exceed America's by 2020. In the words of demographer Nicholas Eberstadt, China "will grow old before it grows rich." The steady flow of Asian investments in American assets, especially U.S. Treasury debt, will reverse as profits must be repatriated home to pay for a growing elderly population.

Democratization

Many of the countries now advancing started with enormous handicaps from failing ideologies. The most prevalent was communism, which held sway over hundreds of millions. With the demise of many authoritarian regimes in the 1990s, their citizens exercised freedom of choice for the first time; and as Adam Smith first pointed out in 1776's *The Wealth of Nations,* one thing that free people choose is to trade. Democratization introduced three billion new capitalists (in economist Clyde Prestowitz's phrase) in Asia to the opportunities available by trading with the West. They will sell their labor in exchange for our technology. The trade made possible by democratization has propelled more people out of poverty in a shorter time than any event in history.

This trend of democratization and globalization has been a boon for the world, lifting billions out of poverty and filling Western stores with cheap goods. But those new capitalists will not be content with low skilled manufacturing jobs: they will climb the value ladder and increasingly compete directly with a growing span of Western industries. Even skilled middle-class professions in the West are under intense competitive pressure. This is one of the main reasons why median incomes in the U.S. have made no real progress for the past few decades.

A Unique Historical Moment

Debt, demographics, and democratization combined to supercharge economic growth in the late 20th century. But simple extrapolation would grossly overestimate our growth prospects in the early 21st century.

Leverage—debt—allows an investor to buy more assets with "other peoples' money" than he could with his funds alone. When those assets rise in value, they boost his returns but when they fall, the debt still must be serviced. This depletes future investments. It may throw them into reverse—disinvestment—when paying down debt becomes the new priority.

In the decades following the high postwar birthrates of the Baby Boom (the mid-1940s to mid-1960s), those countries enjoyed a "demographic dividend": rapidly growing workforces in the 1970s, growing savings from young adults that fueled asset markets in the 1980s, and a productivity boom by experienced workers in the 1990s. But the first decades of the new century will see the inevitable downstroke of this demographic cycle, as workforces shrink and populations age.

Democratization and the globalization that followed have given billions of the poor the means to climb upwards into the global middle class. As their incomes converge with those of advanced countries, most of the low hanging fruit will have been plucked. The most exciting prospect will be in frontier markets that never joined the globalization game or were stifled by authoritarian holdouts from the democratization wave, such as Cuba, North Korea, sub-Saharan Africa, Kazakhstan and most of the Arab world.

In other words, the 1980s through early 2000s (a period called by some economists "Great Moderation," when both unemployment and inflation were low) was the party. The first few decades of the 21st century will be the hangover. At times we may face truly frightening economic prospects, such as 2008–09, when we barely averted Great Depression 2.0. At other times we may grow, but more slowly than past experiences. Some call this "secular stagnation." We call it the "new normal."

A Fragile Financial System

This "new normal" or period of slower economic growth in lower investment returns coincides with the ever increasing fragility of the financial system. The efficient market hypothesis states that individuals may guess asset prices wrong, but the market as a whole gets them right. Most of the time this is correct; however, the financial structure of a capitalist political economy becomes more fragile over a period of prosperity. As the economy grows and profits increase, those businesses in highly profitable areas of the economy are rewarded handsomely for expanding the use of debt. This success encourages others to increase their leverage so as to increase their profits. The increasing profits fuel the creation of credit as lenders are satisfied by the ever increasing profits regarding borrowers' ability to repay the loans.

George Magnus from UBS explains it this way. The stage is first set by "a prolonged period of rapid acceleration of debt" in which more traditional and benign borrowing is steadily replaced by borrowing that depends on new debt to repay existing loans. Then there is the "moment" when lenders become increasingly cautious and restrictive. At this moment it isn't only overleveraged economic units that encounter financing difficulties. At this juncture the risks of systemic economic contraction and asset depreciation become a reality.

Conclusion

Smart investors approaching retirement should turn from a growth focus to an income focus not only due to their own needs, but also due to the realities of the new normal outlined in this chapter. These realities argue strongly for reducing your return ambitions and taking less risk with your investments.

CHAPTER 5

What the New Normal Means for Your Investments

Investors who naively assume the future will be like the past are in for a rude surprise. Smart investors like you know better.

▶ Slower economic growth will mean slower earnings growth, and consequently much more modest returns from stocks. That secret is slowly being acknowledged by investment managers and manifested in higher volatility.

▶ Capital gains will become rarer and smaller. Remember: It's the *income*, stupid! Dividends don't lie: companies can't fake the cash they pay out. Investments that are designed for income, like many alternatives, will grow in popularity.

▶ Although bonds and other fixed income assets like CDs have been retirement staples, their usefulness is much reduced in the new normal. First, interest rates are infinitesimal, so bonds are offering what James Grant calls "return-free risk." Second, after years of debt monetization by central banks, inflation will follow. Any investment (like bonds) that offers a fixed nominal return will get creamed. Interest payments to bondholders will have diminishing purchasing power. As rates rise to compensate for the inflation, they will depress bond prices.

▶ Instead, income should be sought in equity/fixed income hybrids such as alternative investments.

▶ "Alternatives" include both specific asset classes like REITs, MLPs, and BDCs, as well as alternative strategies such as buy/write options and tactical asset allocation. These will be described in Chapters 18 to 22.

▶ Investing in alternatives and pass-through entities offers a double benefit: the high payout ratios they must provide to avoid corporate taxes, and rising prices as more investors seek them out.

▶ Investors in developed countries should overcome their "home bias"—the common proclivity to geographically overweight portfolios toward domestic investments. Stocks in companies headquartered in advanced economies face slowing earnings and significant headwinds from inflation. Increasing your exposure to dynamic developing economies whose favorable demographics help them maintain monetary discipline will earn better returns.

▶ Happily, investing in home country-headquartered firms can still provide some foreign exposure—if the company is a multinational. Companies like Microsoft, Boeing, and Coca-Cola earn well over 50% of their revenues overseas. So with careful stock selection it is possible to enjoy international growth with home country familiarity.

▶ Likewise, all companies are not affected by inflation in the same way. Firms that have pricing power—whose strong competitive position and high market share allow them to raise their prices without seeing a significant loss of customers—can weather inflation, and even prosper from it.

▶ Products that offer principal protection or hedge against longevity will become imperative to mitigate risk.

You should accept that the new normal will provide extra reasons for de-risking your portfolio and migrating portions of it into income-producing assets. But your own personal situation—aging, and your plans to stop working and begin relying on your assets for income—were moving you in this direction already. The balance of this book will explain how to follow through.

PART II

DECUMULATION: THE ENVELOPES APPROACH

CHAPTER 6

The Envelopes Approach

The Envelopes, Please

In Kathryn Forbes' much-loved book, *Mama's Bank Account* (best remembered through the 1948 film *I Remember Mama),* each Saturday evening Papa Lars would bring home his carpenter's pay in coins. Mama Marta would allocate the funds "to the landlord...to the grocer," etc. It is a charming scene.

Most of us do something similar with our savings. We distribute our earnings into "envelopes," or establish mental accounts, that devote pieces of our overall assets to different purposes. We may have, for instance, mental accounts for housing (rent or mortgage), transportation, food, gifts, and luxuries like a vacation. Many households aspire to have a "rainy day" fund for emergencies, although for many it is only a hope.

Each account may be invested differently. An emergency fund envelope should be in a highly liquid form because an illness or layoff may strike at any time. The goal of an emergency fund isn't growth, but capital preservation and immediate access. The same is true for any envelope related to day-to-day spending. A near-term goal envelope may be targeted to a goal that is still a few months or years in the future. For example, a "goal fund" may be used for a house down payment, college tuition, a wedding, or an expensive vacation. A specific mid-term goal envelope, such as for a vacation or a house down payment, can be invested with some growth in mind. However, capital preservation is still important. Finally, a really long-term goal envelope, like retirement savings, can be invested for growth, as long as the long-term goal is still far away. However, as the day approaches when the long-term goal envelope is needed—when that long-term goal becomes a mid-range goal, and then a short-range goal—the investment strategy should change accordingly. A common but outdated rule for really long-term goal funds is that a growing percentage of the portfolio should be in bonds (which are less volatile than stocks, but also return less). That percentage should be roughly equal to the investor's age. Under this guideline, a 58-year old investor saving for retirement should have roughly 58% of his or her retirement savings in bonds. As we've alluded to in previous chapters this is an outdated approach, as much of the research on reverse glide paths illustrates: It's better to glide toward a conservative allocation the closer to retirement you get, and then reversing the process to glide to increasing stock allocation the older you get.

The mental accounts or "envelopes" method is natural for most people. Establishing those accounts literally—that is, investing a portfolio into different components for different time horizons—has also been proven to stretch retirement dollars farther. This chapter will outline this envelopes approach, also known as the "buckets" approach to retirement portfolio construction. It will describe the approach in outline form, briefly mentioning appropriate types of investments for each objective. Further, it will summarize investment research that has demonstrated the superiority of this approach. Much of the remainder of this book is an elaboration of the frame-work introduced in this chapter.

The bucket strategy, what we call the "envelopes approach," was pioneered by the financial advisor Harold Evensky. It's been popularized by some financial planners and also by Christine Benz, the director for personal finance at Morningstar.

Alternatives to Envelopes

There are three ways to construct a retirement portfolio to produce regular income to a retiree: 1) the income generation approach, 2) the systematic withdrawal approach, and 3) the envelopes approach. With the income generation approach, your goal is to keep your principal intact, taking the interest and dividend distributions generated by the portfolio principal as your income. A major drawback of this approach is that your income will fluctuate with varying yields over time. Also, many retirees will need to spend down some or most of their principal to meet their *desired* income needs throughout a long retirement.

Recent studies have indicated that almost two-thirds of retirees use the systematic withdrawal approach, also referred to as the total return approach to income. With this approach the investor has a diversified portfolio of stocks and bonds. Every year, or every six months, you liquidate what you need to spend. You can liquidate proportionately over all the asset classes or different funds you have. Or you can liquidate asset classes that have increased in value the most, like large capitalization stocks, or long-term bonds. The 4% rule described in Chapter 1 is an example.

An Envelope Framework

We are instead proponents of the envelopes approach. The linchpin of the approach is to establish a dedicated safe liquidity pool to provide for your income needs the first few years of retirement. The precise number of envelopes or buckets you need will depend upon the breadth of your financial goals. For retirement planning, the minimum you should consider is two: a long-term growth envelope, and a safe liquid spending envelope with two to three years' worth of cash to meet your spending needs. We will argue that it is better to use at least three envelopes when constructing a retirement portfolio. For shorter term pre-retirement goals, you can expand this approach and proliferate envelopes—at the cost of increased complexity and hassle.

Below is an example of how you could structure an envelope scheme for retirement:

- **Emergency expenses (Envelope 0):** Establish an emergency fund to cover unforeseen contingency expenses. This envelope is separate from the other three envelopes, which are designed to meet your income needs through your retirement. It will be superseded by Envelope 1 once you retire. This envelope consists of cash.

- **Regular spending (Envelope 1):** Throughout your retirement your regular spending will come from Envelope 1. When Envelope 1 is depleted it is refilled with ultraconservative and safe investments. It should include enough cash for approximately two years of normal expenses. Cash or cash equivalents are the core of Envelope 1. Capital preservation is key for investments held in this envelope. Envelope 1 is the source from which regular spending occurs for around five years. (Evensky's original bucket design was 5/5/5—the number of years each bucket covers.)

- **Medium term spending (Envelope 2):** This envelope contains assets you plan to use in the mid-term (the next five to 10 years), invested for stability rather than growth. That is, you take only moderate risk with this envelope. As you approach the fifth year (the end of the investment time horizon for Envelope 1) you will need to start liquidating assets in Envelope 2 to create a new envelope 1.

- **Growth and inflation hedging (Envelope 3):** You have to create a long-term growth envelope. In this envelope you hold assets you don't expect to touch for at least 10 to 15 years. These will be invested for growth and serve as your main hedge against inflation.

Each envelope can use different types of assets. The general idea is that Envelope 0 and most of Envelope 1 should be in very liquid form, such as savings and money market accounts. Envelope 2 should be in short to intermediate duration bond funds. You could include some high quality, income-focused stock investments for a small part of Envelope 2. Envelope 3 should be in illiquid alternatives and stocks (including stock funds and ETFs).

The idea is that you will spend the contents of Envelope 1 for each year that you have planned it (say, five years). At the end of the five-year period you will refill Envelope 1 from Envelope 2. As you approach year 10 (when the assets in Envelope 2 will be depleted), you will refill Envelope 2 by liquidating riskier assets like stock mutual funds in Envelope 3 to reinvest in more moderate assets like bond mutual funds in Envelope 2.

Maintaining the Envelopes

The envelopes approach is a model of simplicity. You determine your time frames for each envelope and segment your investments accordingly, with the very safe investments in Envelope 1, progressing along the risk continuum, sequestering the most volatile and risky investments to Envelope 3, which you don't need to touch for 10-plus years. The foundation of the approach is to maintain a safe, principal-protected pool of assets at all time. Things get a little more complicated when you have to consider how to move assets between the envelopes as the first envelope's assets are spent down.

Before we touch on envelope maintenance we should discuss how the smart investor determines the time frames (time horizons) for each envelope. In the example above we used Evensky's original five-year time frames for each envelope. Your unique circumstances will determine the actual time frames of each envelope. There are a myriad of ways of segmenting the envelopes by time frames as well as by size. Factors that play a role in segmenting are the size of your nest egg relative to the amount of income you wish to generate from your nest egg (the distribution rate or ratio). If your nest egg consists of $1 million and you wish to generate $50,000 per year in inflation-adjusted income for the rest of your life (a 5% distribution rate), you might wish to extend the time frame of Envelope 2 and shorten the time frame of Envelope 1 to increase the proportion of investments with better long-term return potential. At a lower distribution rate there is less pressure on Envelopes 2 and 3 to grow sufficiently to offset the eroding impact of inflation over time.

If you have a large pension and Social Security income making up most of your desired income you could shorten the time frame for Envelopes 1 and 2, taking a little more risk given the stability of your income with an increased Envelope 3 and a shorter period before you need to utilize these growth assets.

If you are more risk averse you would want to increase the time frames as well as sizes of Envelopes 1 and 2 vis-à-vis Envelope 3. Conversely, if you're aggressively inclined you could shorten the time frames of the first two envelopes, or even get rid of Envelope 2 altogether.

Other factors that play a role are longevity or lack thereof, your desire to leave a legacy for your children, and the prevailing economic and capital markets cycle when you commence with your income. Segmenting your envelopes without the help of an advisor can be daunting when you need to refill the envelopes later on. When you've spent Envelope 1 it can be even more intimidating.

According to Christine Benz of Morningstar there are three ways to maintain your envelopes:

▶ *The Mechanical Approach:* Following this approach you move assets from Envelope 2 to 1 and from Envelope 3 to 2 on an annual basis (or some other time period-based frequency).

Your entire portfolio will become progressively more conservative as Envelope 3 shrinks over time (except, of course, if it grows enough to offset the regular liquidations to refill Envelope 2). This approach is simple to understand and execute; however, we believe you should have much longer time periods between refilling than one year. Part of the logic of the envelopes approach is to allow plenty of time for risk assets in Envelope 3 to grow. You don't want to liquidate them during periods of market declines just because it is time to fill Envelope 2.

▶ *The Strict Constructionist Total Return Approach:* According to this approach all income, dividends, and capital gains are reinvested, remaining in their respective envelopes. Periodically you refill envelopes with assets that have appreciated the most. For instance, during strong bull markets you might sell stocks in Envelope 3 to directly refill Envelope 1. During bear markets, Envelope 3 assets are left untouched, refilling Envelope 1 by liquidating bonds in Envelope 2. This implicitly rebalances your total portfolio, which has been proven to offer superior long-run performance.

▶ *The Opportunistic Approach:* We recommend the smart investor follows this eclectic approach in maintaining her envelopes. All income distributions from bonds, stocks, and other investments are automatically transferred to Envelope 1, extending the time frame Envelope 1 can pay you income. During periods of fast-rising interest rates and concomitant declines in bond prices, Envelope 2 interest should be reinvested in the bonds and bond funds in this envelope (achieving escalating interest income). During bear markets, the smart investor should stop transferring dividends and capital gains distributions to Envelope 1 so as to opportunistically reinvest in the declining stocks in Envelope 3, buying at depressed prices. After an extended period of a rising stock market you could consider creaming off some gains to move to either Envelope 1 or 2.

Our Suggested Approach

In our conception of refilling the envelopes we propose that the smart investor focuses first on refilling Envelope 1 with all income distributions from the other two envelopes except when you are opportunistically taking advantage of depressed prices to reinvest. This is a mix of the strict constructionist and opportunistic approaches. When the smart investor approaches the final year of Envelope 1, Envelope 2 assets are liquidated to be shifted into Envelope 1. Every so often you will liquidate highly appreciated assets to move to Envelope 1 and/or 2. Following this approach the smart investor's portfolio will become more aggressive over time (the inverse glide path) as you spend down Envelopes 1 and 2, increasing the percentage of your entire portfolio allocated to Envelope 3. As we discussed earlier, recent research has shown that increasing your equity allocations as you progress through retirement offsets the risks to your portfolio of living longer than anticipated, and allows you to exponentially increase your income later to adjust for inflation. Only when Envelope 2 is fully depleted to fund Envelope 1 will the smart investor liquidate some Envelope 3 assets to recreate new Envelopes 1 and 2, as well as determining new time frames.

Advantages of the Envelopes Approach

There are a number of advantages to the envelopes approach:

1. It smooths your spending in volatile markets. Considerable economic research suggests that "consumption smoothing" is the best way to approach long-term financial planning. (Consumption is what economists call spending.) Milton Friedman won an economics Nobel Prize in part for demonstrating this.

2. Smoother assured income reduces the risk that you will panic and sell in a down market.

3. Drawing down your growth envelope when there is significant appreciation or when Envelope 2 is almost depleted (to refill the downstream buckets) forces periodic rebalancing and reduces the risk that euphoria will keep you in a market bubble too long.

4. Finally, retirement is supposed to be a time without worry. Regularizing your income, to simulate a paycheck, keeps you from losing sleep over market gyrations. Less stress means a longer and happier retired life.

While two-envelope systems are possible (encompassing only Envelopes 1 and 3 in our scheme), in our view that does not really insulate your annual spending from market volatility, and your own impulses. A three-bucket system creates a buffer (Envelope 2) between your long-term Envelope 3 and your liquid Envelope 1, which will act as a shock absorber on your overall spending. The reduced stress may help you live longer.

The Power of Envelopes

A common way to appraise an investing technique is back testing. A portfolio strategy is simulated using historical data on asset returns, to compare its performance with other strategies. Back testing has pitfalls, including hindsight, but it is a reasonably rigorous approach.

There is always a danger that the optimal strategy is an artifact of the historical series used for the back test. Many banks and hedge funds were caught by surprise when housing prices began declining in 2006 because their data series did not extend far enough back to include earlier periods of decline (to the 1930s). To avoid this "data mining" problem, the best back tests randomly select data from their historical database. This approach is called "Monte Carlo" analysis after the famous casino. Commonly, a given strategy is evaluated over thousands of randomized sequences of historical return data, and results reported as a statistical distribution.

In 2010 Morgan Stanley examined several alternative retirement withdrawal strategies under 5,000 Monte Carlo cases. It compared the envelopes approach to other more conventional strategies, and considered withdrawal horizons (the number of years over which withdrawals would occur) of between 30 and 50 years. Similar analyses by Morningstar have also demonstrated the envelopes approach's superiority.

In all cases the envelopes approach—termed "buckets" by Morningstar and "time-segmented baskets" by Morgan Stanley— had the greatest probability of success, preserving some value in the portfolio at the end of the withdrawal period in 95% to 96% of the 5,000 scenarios examined. Other conventional approaches, such as withdrawing a constant amount from an unsegmented portfolio (*a la* Bengen's 4% withdrawal rate), were inferior, but only modestly: successful in 92% to 93% of the Monte Carlo scenarios.

Success better than 19 of 20 times is not a guarantee, but it may reassure you enough to avoid panic selling at the worst times.

Below is a hypothetical envelopes structure for a retired couple summarizing the types of assets suitable for each envelope, and frames the next few chapters.

Hypothetical Envelopes Structure

Retired Couple, ages 62 and 65. $2 million portfolio. Annual income need from portfolio is $70,000 (3.5% withdrawal rate). Increasing the annual income by 4% per year for inflation.

Envelope 1 (Total Amount $375,335)

- ▶ Cash, money market funds, savings accounts: $142,800. This will provide two years' worth of inflation-adjusted income.
- ▶ Certificates of Deposit: $150,645. At 1% annual interest this will grow to $153,673, enough for another two years of inflation-adjusted income in years 3 and 4.

▶ The income need in year 5 will be $81,890. A structured CD or fixed index vehicle issued by insurance companies can be considered for this cash need. These investments are principal-protected, but since you won't know the actual return, for planning purposes we plan for a zero percent return. If it has a positive return it will just stretch out the length of time Envelope 1 provides income.

Envelope 2 (Total Amount $744,898)

▶ Investments in this envelope are made on Day 1 when our hypothetical couple retires (the same time the investments are made in Envelopes 1 and 3).

▶ Envelope 2 is the location for a variable annuity with a protected income base (which we will discuss in more detail later). Placing $400,000 in such a vehicle, assuming a 5% guaranteed growth rate of the income base, the total at the end of year 5 would be $510,513. Assuming an annual lifetime income based on a 4.5% distribution rate, it would be $22,973 starting in year 6 for life.

▶ Basket of bond funds: $200,000.

▶ Income-focused fund with bonds and dividend-paying stocks: $144,898.

▶ Envelope 2's investments paying interest, dividends, or capital gains distributions won't be reinvested at this stage. Rather, the income distributions will pour into Envelope 1. We assume a yield of 2.5% annually on these investments pouring into Envelope 1 from the basket of bond funds and the income-focused funds holding both bonds and dividend-paying stocks. Dividends, interest, and capital gains distributions generated within the variable annuity are reinvested inside the VA (variable annuity). With Envelope 2's cash distributions flowing into Envelope 1 and after each year being reinvested in a CD earning 1.5% interest, our couple will have $44,425 built up in this envelope.

Envelope 3 (Total Amount $879,767):

▶ This is the couple's long-term growth envelope. The investments in this envelope won't be needed for 10-plus years. This envelope should focus on stock market investments and alternative investments (alts). The remainder of the $2 million is invested in this envelope.

▶ We again follow the approach of not reinvesting dividends, interest, or capital gains distributions, instead pouring them into Envelope 1. If we assume a 1.74% yield from the investments in Envelope 3, $15,286 will pour into Envelope 1 each year, reinvested in CDs at 1.5%. The total at the end of year 5 will be $78,756.

▶ The decision to pour income distributions into Envelope 1 or to reinvest them in their respective envelopes will be determined tactically based on the capital market cycles.

Outline of the First 10 Years for the Hypothetical Couple

Year	Age	Income	Source
1	62/65	$70,000	Cash/money market/savings in Envelope 1
2	63/66	$72,800	Cash/money market/savings in Envelope 1
3	64/67	$75,712	Maturing CD in Envelope 1
4	65/68	$78,740	Maturing CD in Envelope 1
5	66/69	$81,890	Maturing structured product in Envelope 1
6	67/70	$85,166	Annuity provides $22,973. Dividends and interest payments from Envelopes 2 and 3 compounded at 1.5% over 4 years (it poured into Envelope 1 and was invested in CDs at 1.5%). It now totals $123,181. Need: $85,166 − $22,973 (annuity) = $62,193 remaining need, taken from $123,181. This leaves $60,988 in cash from matured CDs.
7	68/71	$88,573	Need: $88,573 − $22,973 (annuity) = $65,600 (remaining need). $60,988 cash remained from the previous year. Added to this cash all Envelope 2 and 3 income distributions during year 6 ($23,520). Taking the $65,600 remaining need from this accumulated cash. Leaving $18,908. At the end of year 7 we assume a major stock market decline takes place. Going forward, dividends from Envelope 3 are reinvested.

8	69/72	$92,115	Need: $92,115 − $22,973 (annuity) = $69,142 remaining need. Interest from Envelope 2 is $8,622 added to the cash of $18,908 ($27,530). Leaving a need of $41,612 after using all the cash. At this stage the couple will liquidate the bond funds. We assume they liquidate for the original amount invested of $200,000 (at par). $200,000 − $41,612 leaves $158,388 in cash.
9	70/73	$95,800	Need: $95,800 − $22,973 (annuity) = $72,827 remaining need. Cash is $158,388 plus interest, dividends, and capital gains distributions at an assumed 2.5% rate of remaining Envelope 2 investments ($3,622). Total cash $158,388 plus $3,622 = $162,010. Taking the remaining need ($72,827) leaves $89,183.
10	71/74	$99,632	Need: $99,632 − $22,973 (annuity) = $76,659 remaining need. Cash is $89,183 plus new income distributions of $3,622 = $92,805. Taking remaining need leaves $16,146 ($92,805 − $76,659). We now use Envelope 3 investments and recreate 3 new Envelopes, liquidating the remaining Envelope 2 investments to fund a new Envelope 1.

If we assume no capital growth on the Envelope 2 remaining income-oriented funds because their interest, dividends, and capital gains poured into Envelope 1 over the last year, the amount remaining in Envelope 2 is $144,898. There is still $16,146 remaining in Envelope 1 cash. The $400,000 variable annuity is still available to provide $22,973 in annual lifetime income.

Interest, dividends, and capital gains distributions from Envelope 3 investments poured into Envelope 1 for the first 7 years after which it was reinvested. If we assume a compounded growth (capital appreciation) of 4% on all Envelope 3 assets for 10 years (very conservative), then Envelope 3 could total $1,302,270. Add to this the Envelope 1 and 2 remaining amounts (excluding the variable annuity) and the total for recreating the envelopes could be $1,463,314.

The remaining investment value (lump sum) of the variable annuity will depend on the growth of the underlying investments minus the withdrawals that started in year 6. To make the math simple let's assume the underlying investments achieved a 5.5% total return each year. This will leave the remaining investment value of the variable annuity at $547,991. Hypothetically, at this stage, the total portfolio of our couple could be $2,011,305.

Of course, one can pick this hypothetical example apart, and reality will probably be different. But it gives the smart investor some idea of how an envelopes structure could function.

CHAPTER 7

Envelopes 0 and 1
. . . .
Safe Assets

Note: This book is about the life stage when you have chosen to no longer have a regular paycheck from work, so no need for an income bridge until you find a new job. You are retired, and do not plan another job. Therefore, we discuss Envelope 0—the emergency fund—only briefly. For those still working, however, we believe an emergency fund (Envelope 0) should be your top priority.

How Much?

One of the highest priorities smart investors undertake is to create an emergency fund. An unexpected, unavoidable expense due to illness or accident can be life-altering. About 60% of bankruptcies involve unplanned medical bills.

Even if you are fortunate enough to be very healthy, your employer may not be. Even in very stable occupations, bouts of unemployment are common. More than one in 15 college-educated workers lose their jobs in any given year under a normal economy. This proportion jumps in recessions.

Financial advisors once advised clients to keep three to six months of expenses in an emergency fund. If your after-tax household income was $50,000 per year, and you spent $45,000, an emergency fund of $11,250 to $22,500 was considered prudent to insulate you from most crises, medical or economic. The logic was that health and disability insurance would apply after a deductible or waiting period, and most jobseekers returned to work within a few months. Both those sanguine assumptions were invalidated by the Great Recession. We argue for much more protection: you should have *at least* six months but a full year would be safer.

Keeping a year's worth of expenses in liquid form is a necessary habit for the day when you will not have a paycheck, by design—when you will be retired. You cannot spend stocks or bonds, only cash, so the idea is to plan your conversion of assets from illiquid to liquid on a schedule based on your needs and expenses. Otherwise, your need for funds may occur during a market drop. That is the logic behind an emergency fund: the loss of your paycheck may well coincide with declining asset prices if both are caused by an economic downturn.

The right size for Envelope 0 will vary greatly over your life cycle. In the early stages of your career, it should be your first priority. As your income rises with career experience, you should limit growth in your expenses to a lower rate (say, half as fast). Since your reserve fund is sized to one year's worth of expenses, not income, it need not rise as fast as your income—if you keep your expenses in check. Once you have successfully accumulated assets, by near retirement you should have between 15 and 25 times a year's expenses in your portfolio, so your reserve fund may be only 5% to 10% as much. Then in retirement, savings will cease, and your portfolio could stop growing. As it eventually shrinks due to withdrawals for spending, if you refill your reserve fund each year it will occupy a growing portfolio share. Financially, you will have come full circle.

Envelope 0 and most of Envelope 1, which exist to replace a paycheck when it disappears—by surprise in your working years

(Envelope 0), and by design in retirement (Envelope 1)—should be in highly liquid form, such as a savings account or a money market fund. Your main goals are accessibility and stable value. Growth is a goal for other envelopes.

Idle Money

The most common argument against a large reserve fund is that those funds are "idle money" and their value will not grow. This has long been true for checking accounts, but today it is also true for most interest-bearing short-term investments such as T-bills or commercial paper, and the money market funds that invest in them. The Fed's intense efforts to "financially repress" interest rates have made all interest-bearing assets unappealing, especially those of the shortest maturities.

But the stability of these asset classes is exactly what you should seek for your short-term paycheck replacement. Without the liquid/ stable value Envelopes 0 and 1, you would need to sell volatile assets every time you had an expense. When the market is strong, you might need to sell 100 shares; after a drop, you might need to sell 300. A few down markets might persuade you to exit the market entirely and stay exclusively in cash. This would *permanently* sacrifice the long-term growth potential of stocks. Envelope 1 allows you to avoid worrying about market gyrations affecting mostly Envelope 3 investments, since you won't need to touch them for around 10 years. Think of Envelope 1 not as idle money but as a net worth and consumption *smoother* that allows most of your portfolio to keep working for you.

Where to Invest Envelopes 0 and 1

There are generally two types of investments suitable for covering your annual fixed expenses: (a) short-term interest-bearing investments and (b) annuities, specifically three types—single premium immediate annuities (SPIA's), fixed annuities, and fixed index annuities. Some advisors might suggest other types of investment vehicles for Envelopes 0 and 1; however, our approach is to try and avoid the risk of price declines of the contents of these envelopes. Principal protection is essential. Smart investors shouldn't be forced into the untenable position of having to sell an investment at a loss to meet current income needs.

Annuities for Envelope 1

There is considerable confusion amongst the investment public when it comes to the term "annuity." An "annuity" is a stream of regular income. However, there are many varieties of annuities, and the smart investor should be able to distinguish among them. Bear in mind, the term "annuity" is very generic. It can be compared to the term "vehicle." There is a wide variety of "vehicles" we use for transport. There are skates, bicycles, motorcycles, cars, ships, trains, etc. In the same vein the differences among annuities are as wide. Lumping them all together is reductionist and simplistic.

Short-Term Fixed Income Investments

As mentioned earlier, a traditional retirement strategy was a "ladder" of CDs or short-term bonds (with maturities of less than five years), staggered at successive maturity dates—say, every three or six months. When one matured and your principal was returned to you, you would deposit it in a more liquid form like a money market account. Any unspent funds would be used to purchase a new short-term security with the next maturity date on your ladder.

Money market funds use a similar strategy within the fund, saving you the expense and management headaches of laddering short-term securities yourself—and offering the diversification possible by pooling the funds of millions of investors.

At the time this is written, and probably for the foreseeable future, traditional bricks-and-mortar banks are offering only a few basis points (hundredths of a percent) in annual interest on savings accounts, and generally barely 1% per year on CDs. (To calibrate small differences in interest rates, bankers use the term "basis points"—1/100th of one percent is one basis point. So the difference between 0.75% and 0.50% is 25 basis points.) Internet-based banks, which avoid the fixed costs of a branch structure, may offer a slightly higher rate. Many Internet banks meet FDIC requirements, so each account is FDIC-insured up to its per-account maximum ($250,000 at this writing; previously $100,000). Many retirees spread their reserve fund over several banks and accounts so that all of it is FDIC-insured.

By establishing Envelopes 0 and 1, the smart investor can avoid incurring a loss or penalty when liquidating an investment vehicle to pay for an emergency or to meet an income need in retirement. Savings accounts and money market funds are easily accessible without the risk of loss of principal when liquidating. This is an important consideration given the current low interest rate environment, since bond prices decline as interest rates rise. (The size of the decline is related to the maturity of the bond.) Although you can always sell a bond in your ladder in the open market, the prevailing market price could be less than what you paid for it. Likewise, liquidating a CD before maturity incurs a penalty.

Money market funds and CDs are core investment vehicles for Envelopes 0 and 1—they incur no penalties or decline of value for early withdrawal—but they lack FDIC protection unless issued by an FDIC-insured bank. The "breaking of the buck"—the fall in money markets' net asset value below its targeted $1 per share in the summer of 2008—was one of the dramatic early events that led to the financial industry meltdown and subsequent government bailout. The federal government extended its credit guarantees temporarily to money market funds during the crisis—an acknowledgment of Americans' pervasive dependence on them for liquidity.

A portion of the smart investor's Envelope 1 assets could be allocated to obtain a bit higher yield by using mutual funds that invest in short-term bonds (although we prefer bond investments to be held in Envelope 2). For Envelope 1, you should restrict your consideration to *very* short-term bond funds—funds that invest in interest-bearing assets that mature within months to a very few years. Mutual funds offer diversification, and managers who (in theory) can maneuver in the face of rapidly changing interest rates. Mutual funds are fully liquid, trading in high volumes on major exchanges—closed-end funds trade at the market, and open-end funds once a day. But you cannot access them as easily as through a bank ATM, so traditional bank accounts are still needed for immediate transactions. Mutual funds will be discussed extensively in a later chapter.

Structured Products

Structured products are principal-protected securities whose payments are linked to a major stock market index or other type of benchmark. These securities are fixed interest-bearing investments, but unlike a traditional fixed investment with a declared interest rate and maturity, these securities don't have a declared fixed interest rate. They offer an unknown interest rate based on the reference index performance. There are various types of structured products created by investment banks. Those that have FDIC insurance are called structured CDs; those without FDIC insurance are referred to as structured notes. These products are liquid since they trade in the bond market, but their prices could be a little more volatile than short-term bonds since the interest credit method is based on the performance of a more volatile reference index. If you hold them till maturity they are principal protected—their return can never be negative.

These securities have more upside potential than other fixed-income securities. In exchange for the upside, you give up some performance since these vehicles are either capped to only a certain percentage of the index performance, or you only receive credit above a certain threshold.

Pensions and Pension-like Products Such as Single Premium Immediate Annuities (SPIAs)

The closest equivalent to a paycheck is a pension. Once upon a time, many employers offered them to longstanding employees. You could expect a monthly payment whose amount was based on your age, wages when working, and years of service with the company. Pensions were designed to reward and induce loyalty. Generally, pension payments were fixed for your natural life—a common pension might provide 40% or 50% of your final working income. Unlike wages, which may rise if there is competition among employers for skilled labor, pensions were fixed in nominal dollars. Inflation eroded those dollars, so workers who retired in the 1940s on a pension of $200 per month saw their middle-class lifestyle descend into poverty in the 1970s when inflation cut that payment's purchasing power by two-thirds.

Pensions are a bargain employers make with employees. Not only will the employees receive some of their compensation in a deferred form (a pension), but the employees/retirees *do not bear investment risk;* the employer does. Their employer has committed to providing a "defined benefit"—a scheduled payment. This payment does not change, regardless of gyrations in the markets where pension fund assets are invested. If investment returns aren't enough to meet the defined benefit schedule, employers must contribute more to the pension fund to backfill.

By the high inflation 1970s, senior executives in some companies realized that their expected pension benefits were not keeping up with inflation. They wanted to compensate by saving more in tax advantaged accounts, but existing vehicles like IRAs had income and contribution ceilings. Firms lobbied for the creation of a tax-advantaged savings program for these executives, and the 401(k) plan was born. Such plans are termed "defined contribution" in contrast to pensions' "defined benefit" because contributions (whether by the employee, employer, or both) were associated with a specific employee. They are a tax-advantaged investment account that is not tied to any employer; it is "portable" when the employee changes jobs. Congress required that the same deal be available to all employees.

Within a few years, employers realized the advantages—to them—of defined contribution plans over defined benefit pensions: employers shed investment risk. More accurately, they offloaded the risk onto their employees and retirees. In the early days of defined contribution plans, employers encouraged savings by their employees by offering to match them up to a ceiling (typically between 3% and 6% of salary). Employers might not reduce their costs much in the short run (versus their previous contribution to pension funds) if employees took full advantage of the match. But shedding long-term risk also had value. And few employees contributed much to their plans, so employer-matching contributions were far less than to defined benefit pension plans.

By the 1980s, some employers had let their defined benefit pension plans fade away through attrition, enrolling new employees only in defined contribution plans. Today less than one in five employees can expect a pension. Almost all of them are in government; very few private sector employers still offer pensions to new employees.

Pensions are like paychecks in their predictability. But paychecks can grow when the company prospers; pensions do not. Social Security uses current payroll taxes to pay current retiree benefits, and is indexed to inflation, but most private pensions are not. However, the general consumer price index does not fully capture the higher rate of inflation that senior citizens experience, as noted earlier.

At least a portion of your retirement spending may come from a pension—the universal one known as Social Security. If you have not done so before, review the annual statement you receive from the Social Security Administration estimating your annual payment in retirement, or use the calculators at www.ssa.gov. For many it is a sobering experience, because it confirms that the program was designed to protect the elderly from poverty, not to fund a generous spending pattern. The exercise will also demonstrate the value of delaying the start of your collection of Social Security payments, if possible until age 70. This will be discussed briefly in a later chapter.

For many of us, projected Social Security payments will provide a respectable fraction of our minimum expenses—but only a fraction, perhaps 20% to 40%. (For the bottom 60% of households it provides the majority of their retirement income.) This builds a base for Envelope 1, and it has implications for the other envelopes also.

A Single Premium Immediate Annuity (SPIA) is like a pension you can purchase from an insurance company. You pay an insurance company a lump sum, and based on your age and sex the insurance company contractually commits to pay you an income stream (either monthly, annually, or quarterly) for the rest of your life.

Fixed Annuities and Fixed Index Annuities

Fixed annuities are a type of deferred annuity, meaning income is being deferred for a period of time. A fixed annuity is comparable to a bond, or a bank certificate of deposit. It is almost an insurance company CD, but without FDIC insurance. The investor commits his money for a certain period, typically between four and seven years at the conclusion of which the fixed annuity term has progressed beyond its surrender period. In bond or CD speak, the fixed annuity "matured." Unlike a traditional CD, where the interest is declared for the entire period, most insurance companies issuing fixed annuities declare the interest rate each year, which cannot go below a contractual minimum. This type of variable interest crediting is advantageous in a rising rate environment.

Another type of annuity you can utilize in Envelope 1 is a fixed index annuity (FIA). Like a fixed annuity a FIA is a deferred annuity where the investor defers taking income until sometime in the future. However, instead of the insurance company declaring an interest credit each year the interest is credited by using some reference index like the S&P 500, or the Dow Jones Industrial Average. There are many varieties of fixed index annuities which also differ in complexity. A fixed index annuity is the insurance world's equivalent of structured CD and structured notes. The different types of annuities are discussed in more detail in Chapter 12.

Target Amounts for Annuitized Income

In the spirit of the envelopes approach, you should organize your portfolio so that enough income can be generated from stable assets to cover your fixed, mandatory expenses. Let's say that of your expected $80,000 per year in spending, $50,000 will be needed for fixed expenses and $30,000 for discretionary/variable expenses. Ideally $50,000 of income should come from pension-like sources. Say that you expect Social Security to provide you $27,000 per year in income. You could set a goal of $23,000 per year to come from annuities.

Insurance companies pay agents and financial advisors generous commissions to sell these profitable products. So it isn't surprising to find some unethical salesmen persuading clients to buy far more than is prudent. For example, an 85-year-old is unlikely to earn a positive return on a lifetime annuity. Financial advisors generally argue that SPIAs should not absorb more than about 25% of your portfolio.

We agree, but we state it as follows:

- ▶ Make single premium immediate annuities (private pension annuities) a minority of your portfolio, because in Envelope 3 you will need assets to grow and hedge against inflation.
- ▶ Target an amount that tops off your fixed expenses, after Social Security and pensions. (This was $23,000 per year in the example above.)
- ▶ Set the non-annuity side of Envelope 1 in light of your annuity and pension income. If you expect to have $4,000 per month in expenses, and pension-like income will generate $3,500 per month, then you need maintain only $6,000 to $12,000 ($500 per month x 12 to 24 months) in liquid form.

Effect on Other Envelopes

York University professor Moshe Milevsky's wonderful book *Are You a Stock or a Bond?* points out that your portfolio's allocation among assets should not be based on your tolerance for risk only—the subject of countless advisors' questionnaires—but also on the riskiness of your income sources. The more volatile your working income the more stable your portfolio should be—i.e., lower risk. Working for a world dominator company like Intel, J&J, or Microsoft is far less risky than for a small startup. Having protected employment due to tenure or civil service status is even less so. You can dial up the risk in your future income (i.e., your retirement savings) if your present income (your paycheck) is at low risk.

Likewise, the larger your stream of stable income that flows into Envelope 1 (such as government pensions and annuitized income), the more risk you can take in Envelope 3.

Envelopes 0 and 1 Summary

You should keep at least one year's worth of minimum (fixed) expenses on hand in liquid form for emergencies while you are earning a paycheck. The same logic applies in retirement, although you may wish to raise it to two to three years. Now your "paycheck" will come from Envelope 1, and having funds there will save you from the obligation to sell into a market downturn to meet day to day expenses.

Chances are good that a fair fraction of what you need for Envelope 1 will get refilled every year already, through Social Security. You can supplement this pension with pension-like income streams such as single premium immediate annuities (SPIAs). The more income you get from pension-like sources, the more risk you can afford to take with the rest of your assets. That is, a large pension share in Envelope 1 allows you to overweight Envelope 3.

Investments that work well for Envelope 1 are money market funds, CDs, structured CDs and notes, SPIAs, fixed annuities, and fixed index annuities.

CHAPTER 8

Envelope 3

Growth and Inflation Hedging

Now that we explained Envelopes 0 and 1, before we address Envelope 2, we want to address Envelope 3, which is the focus of most writing about retirement savings. The classic advice, as noted in Chapter 3, is to weight your portfolio heavily in stocks or stock funds in your early years, gradually reweighted towards more stable investments like bonds and bond funds as retirement approaches. Most financial advisors believe that some allocation to stocks is necessary even in retirement, so that your nominal income can grow to counterbalance inflation's dilution of its purchasing power.

As noted in earlier chapters, this basic philosophy remains unquestioned, but the specifics need to change. Bond prices are being levitated by central banks. When quantitative easing ends, their antigravity machines will flicker off.

Given long lifespans and the length of time people will spend in retirement compared to previous generations, having an Envelope 3 is an important strategy to protect against the eroding effects of inflation on retirees' purchasing power. Although the smart investor needs to reweight towards the stability of bonds and other less volatile investments, reducing the absolute size of Envelope 3 as the smart investor progresses through retirement, Envelope 3 should remain significant or even grow vis-à-vis the other envelopes to help hedge against inflation as the smart investor ages. The smart investor decreases his allocation to stocks and other risky investments the closer he gets to commence taking income out of his portfolio. As Envelopes 1 and 2 are spent down the proportion of Envelope 3 will slowly increase as a percentage of his entire portfolio. This is "reverse" or "inverse" glide path.

Inflation Hedges

Hard Assets and Commodities

Traditionally, hard assets like real estate and commodities have been the most common inflation hedges. Gold bugs argue that when paper currencies' value evaporates (i.e., under inflation), gold's value endures. Similar arguments are made for silver, platinum, rare earths, gemstones, energy, cropland, and agricultural products like soybeans, corn, or beef, and timberland. In inflationary periods gurus will tout "systems" of heavily leveraged bets on commodity prices using options or future contracts. Collectibles such as stamps, coins, art, or comic books also come into vogue under high inflation.

All of these ideas are *speculations* on future prices, not *investments* in productive (competitive) businesses. There are no low-risk commodity bets; commodities are intensely cyclical. High prices will encourage expanded production, which will cause prices to crash. Low prices will drive producers out of business, creating shortages that drive prices up.

We believe that commodity *producers* merit a very small place in your Envelope 3. Unlike the commodity they produce, the companies actually generate earnings—as they must in order to attract capital in a competitive environment. Competition drives performance in this industry as in every other. But commodity producers are first of all *stocks*, and risky ones at that.

Stocks and Stock Funds

The basic problem with stocks is, of course, volatility. Superior returns come only from superior risk. While in your 20s and 30s you can be blasé about risk because your investing horizon when you need the money is still decades away, your "risk tolerance" will probably shrink drastically when time is no longer on your side. The challenge, then, will be: *How to enjoy most of the returns of stocks, but modulate the risks?*

Wall Street's marketing machine offers a number of answers—from newsletters, to mutual funds, to outright snake oil. This book provides three proven approaches. First, the *envelopes* approach assures that the funds you need for the next five to seven years are insulated from market swings, because they are invested in stable assets. Second, the *portfolio* perspective offers ideas for assets that have low or negative correlations with stocks. Finally, we recommend a larger-than-customary allocation to a class of assets known by a singularly unrevealing name: *alternative investments*. They are so named because they are neither bonds nor stocks.

Stocks and stock funds will continue to be the most important component of the smart investor's Envelope 3 holdings. They are discussed in Chapters 11 and 14.

Alternative Investments

There are a wide range of "alternative investments," from hedge funds to managed futures, which should be part of the smart investor's Envelope 3 assets. The income-focused smart investor should focus on alternatives that serve as intermediate points on the spectrum between pure-growth investments (such as small cap stocks) and pure-income investments (such as government bonds)—so-called *hybrid* alternatives. Their hybrid nature offers three important advantages:

▶ Many hybrid alternatives offer generous yields, frequently two to four times that of high dividend stocks. Often this is legally required to avoid corporate taxes, as for real estate investment trusts (REITs), business development companies (BDCs), and master limited partnerships (MLPs). These dividends reduce your need to sell assets to generate income, offering both management and tax advantages.

▶ Due to their high income generation, hybrid alternatives could be less volatile than stocks. We want to emphasize *could*—there will be periods when hybrids experience volatility; this volatility is smoothed by the high income they generate.

▶ Some of these alternatives have low correlations with stock indexes and bonds, so including them in your portfolio could further smooth fluctuations. One class that many may not be familiar with is nontraded versions of common alternatives such as REITs and BDCs, which are priced through a different pricing mechanism than traded stocks, contributing to their correlation advantage. The distinction between traded and nontraded investments is explored in Chapter 16.

The range of assets appropriate for Envelope 3 is vast, and markets change constantly, so we will not recommend specific investments. Later chapters in Part III dealing with these assets will open your thinking to the range of possibilities. Part III offers comments about each, including their warts.

International Stocks and Bonds

Our previous book *Your Macroeconomic Edge* argued that long-term economic prospects in developed economies are handicapped by *demographics* and *debt*. At the same time the economic prospects of the developing world are rising due to *democratization* that has allowed these countries to take advantage of globalization. This argues for overweighting foreign investments in Envelope 3.

Many investors do the opposite, due to significant "home bias": They overweight in geographies or industries familiar to them. International investing requires overcoming home bias. In many countries the added risk is not from inferior investor protection—most countries recognize that such protections are necessary to attract foreign capital. The main added risk is currency fluctuations. If the home currency of the foreign stock in which you invest dives, its earnings will exchange into fewer dollars. Even strong "own currency" earnings growth may be poor dollar growth. Positive returns can even become negative if exchange rates move a great deal.

While we are long-term bears on developed country currencies, including the dollar, we recognize that there can be major crosscurrents at any given time. For instance, every crisis provokes a "flight to safety," which for the present generally still means dollars. Therefore, while we recommend moderately overweighting your overall portfolio in foreign investments or in U.S. companies earning significant revenue in the emerging world, particularly in demographically-favored emerging countries, we suggest restricting those investments to Envelope 3.

The Special Case of Real Estate

Real estate is the most common holding in many investors' portfolios. For many Americans, equity in their owner-occupied home is the largest asset on their balance sheet. Millions of people have also become landlords, usually owning rental properties in nearby neighborhoods. The housing bust in 2008 offered new opportunities to buy income-generating real estate directly. This asset class can be a very useful Envelope 3 element, but with special caveats.

Real estate is a promising investment in an area with good economic fundamentals—that is, with economic and population growth. This is because an investor can turbocharge returns with leverage. Think of your own home. If you made a 20% down payment, you borrowed 80% of the purchase price from other peoples' money. Every 1% change in your house's price changed the value of your equity by 5%. This is true whether prices rise or fall— that's why it is called "leverage"—so late 2000s price crash devastated many homeowners. Despite the expression "safe as houses," a leveraged house is rarely low risk.

In addition, for most individual investors, buying properties directly is the opposite of diversified. Buildings are expensive, so your portfolio will be highly concentrated. You will almost certainly buy in the region where you live, so your real estate holdings will also be concentrated geographically, and they will be highly correlated with one another. Real Estate Investment Trusts (REITs), by contrast, offer a way to own diversified real estate in a fund-like vehicle.

Finally, regardless of the benefit to your personal balance sheet of a valuable primary residence, *that value is strictly theoretical unless you move out*. Selling or renting it out unlocks some or all of your equity. But you will need a new residence. Borrowing against the equity to remain in your home may be possible and even attractive at current ultralow interest rates, but it increases your leverage. You may take more risk than you intend. (We omit reverse mortgages, whose terms are far less attractive than traditional mortgages, and home equity lines of credit as outside of our scope.)

Our view on real estate: you can earn superior returns by buying and managing properties yourself. But your time and hassle may burden you more than fees you would otherwise pay a manager. Consider the long-term prospects of the region. You may already be overexposed through the home you occupy. And your residence isn't really a portfolio asset, although it shows up on your personal balance sheet. If you want more real estate exposure, the better (more diversified) way to gain it is through REITs.

Envelope 3 Summary

Most of the knowledge you acquired to become a smart investor that served you so well in your accumulation stage will apply well to Envelope 3. This envelope should always be relatively heavy in stocks or stock funds to hedge against inflation and allow some growth in retirement to counteract depletions from withdrawals—although these withdrawals could be less than conventional wisdom due to the realities of the new normal. Diversification remains important, as does keeping management costs low (e.g., through indexed mutual funds and ETFs).

Since you will hold the assets in Envelope 3 the longest, it is particularly important to focus on how they correlate with stocks, and with each other. Many alternative assets offer good income that dampens their volatility and lowers their correlation with stocks.

Real estate can be a promising Envelope 3 asset, but it is easy to overdo it. Leverage is a key investment advantage in up markets, and a killer in declining markets. Your home is only a financial asset if you move out, or if you increase leverage to dangerous levels. Direct ownership of real estate near your home will entail effort and hassles that you must consider part of your cost, and it will probably overconcentrate you in a single asset class and geography. We favor instead the diversification made possible through REITs.

CHAPTER 9

Envelope 2

. . . .

Medium Term Spending, Moderate Risk Assets

If you want to keep things as simple as possible, Envelopes 1 and 3 will do the trick. (Envelope 0 is a given. Build it first.) But you will need to refill Envelope 1 by liquidating (selling) assets from Envelope 3 every few years. Bear markets often last longer than that. The imperative of generating Envelope 1 money so often may lead you to sell Envelope 3 assets at imprudent times, buying high and selling low. A shock absorber can help you restrain your worst impulses. That is the purpose of Envelope 2.

This envelope is the mid-term bridge between the shorter term Envelope 1 and long-term Envelope 3. You should fill it with investments that you plan to use when Envelope 1 assets are close to being depleted. Envelope 2 assets will have a time horizon of between five years and 10 years. Examples include:

▶ **Income mutual funds:** These include funds that invest in bonds that mature in five to 10 years (called "mid duration"), as well as high dividend stock funds.

▶ **Fixed index annuities:** This type of annuity can be used in either Envelope 1 or 2. See the chapter discussing Envelope 1 investments and Part III for an explanation of how these vehicles function.

▶ **Variable annuities with living benefit riders:** "Living benefit riders" are optional additions to a deferred variable annuity that guarantee that the value of your accumulated premiums cannot go below a specified threshold, even if the underlying investment funds decline in value. There is a lump-sum value and a protected income base which is paid out to the investor as a lifetime income stream. Unlike a single premium immediate annuity, this type of annuity allows the investor access and control of the underlying investments while receiving income. When the investor does not take income, the protected income base increases by a certain percentage or the market gains of the underlying funds, whichever is greater. We will discuss these vehicles in detail in later chapters when we provide an overview of the investment vehicles suitable for Envelopes 2 and 3.

▶ **Return of principal annuities:** This is a type of variable annuity where the insurance company insures the underlying fund investments against market loss over a certain period of time. It differs from a variable annuity with a living benefit rider in the sense that the guaranteed amount (which is typically the original investment) is paid out in a lump sum after a certain term.

▶ **Buy/write stock funds:** Options on stocks were originally created to allow stockholders to manage risks. For example, buying a call option allows the holder to "call away" a stock at its strike price. Exercising the option on a stock that has risen above the strike price buys the stock at a discount to its current price. Buy/write funds sell options such as calls, earning the option premium, which is immediate income. (Calls on stock you already own are "covered"; calls on stock you do not own are "naked." If the buyer of the naked call option you sold exercises it, you will be obliged to buy the stock at the market price so that you can meet your obligation to sell it to the option holder at the strike price.) Such funds earn higher income than from stock dividends alone, at the price of giving up some upside, since it will be called away if the stock rises above its strike price. These are time-consuming strategies are discussed in Chapter 21. The smart investor might be better served investing in mutual funds that follow buy/write strategies.

As you progress in your retirement it is likely that the risk level associated with Envelope 2 will come to be about as much as you wish to take. Slowly draining Envelope 3 to overfill Envelope 2 is a very common strategy. (But do it methodically, not in a panic, which you will later regret.) Due to the prospect of higher future inflation, which is usually magnified for senior citizens, we recommend always keeping some assets in Envelope 3 growth investments.

Envelope 2 Summary

This envelope is the shock absorber. It allows you to refill Envelope 1 on a schedule of your choosing when Envelope 1 gets close to being depleted. This should moderate the queasy feelings that are only natural in a market meltdown, because you know that you can wait several years (long enough for stocks to recover) before you need to sell Envelope 3 assets. Envelope 2 can refill Envelope 1 without trauma, because Envelope 2 holds several years' worth of assets that typically absorb market downturns far better than stocks.

The price of this envelope is extra effort and management. You could manage with only Envelopes 1 and 3, but without the shock absorption capacity. That's why we recommend all three envelopes. But if you prefer to skip Envelope 2, you can compensate by:

▶ Taking a bit less risk in Envelope 3, including growth assets as a minor share.

▶ Increasing the size of Envelope 1 to cover a longer period of time. This is easiest if you expect considerable income from pension-like assets in Envelope 1 so that the cash you must add is a minor part.

For More Information

Part III contains a series of chapters describing each asset class and investment vehicle in more detail, and provides unvarnished commentary on their strengths and weaknesses in the context of the envelopes approach. It is designed as a reference: We hope you will return to it often as you readjust your portfolio.

PART III

A GUIDE TO INVESTMENT CHOICES

Introduction to Part III

Part III consists of twelve chapters that introduce and explain some of the major investment options open to you in the context of the envelopes approach. Each is designed as a resource that you can refer back to when you need it; for example, when an advisor pitches an investment to you. We definitely are not neutral about some of these. We have our opinions and do not hold back. More space is given to investments that may be less familiar to you, such as most "alternatives," with standard options such as CDs, bonds, and stocks treated much more briefly.

These short chapters are meant only as introductions to each asset class. This book's resources section suggests a few other sources that can help you delve deeper into any asset type that interests you. We also do not make any specific recommendations because market conditions change rapidly, so any suggestions would be obsolete before this book reaches you.

While we make a few comments regarding the suitability of some options to particular readers' goals, we cannot offer individual advice in a book. We encourage you to arm yourself through this education so that you can meet your advisor on even terms.

CHAPTER 10

Traditional Options I

· · · · · · · · · ·

Savings Accounts, Money Market Funds, CDs, Bonds, and Bond Mutual Funds (Envelope 1 and Envelope 2)

All assets can be arrayed on a spectrum of risk and return. As a very general principle with many exceptions, the less risky your investment, the lower the return you can expect compared to other possibilities. Envelope 1 is intended for about five years of expenses, including for potential emergencies. Liquidity and stability, not high return, is the priority. A core holding in Envelope 1 is very short-term interest-bearing instruments.

Savings Accounts

Before the Internet, the primary distinction among bank accounts was between checking and savings. The first allowed you to draw on deposited funds at any time and place, by issuing a receipt—writing a check—that your counterparty could present to your bank.

Checking accounts were the most convenient, and they typically paid no interest. Savings accounts required the depositor to physically enter a bank branch with proof of their deposit—usually a "passbook"—to withdraw funds. This extra hurdle made savings accounts marginally less liquid, allowing banks to offer interest. For many of us our first encounter with the banking system was when we opened a passbook savings account as a young child.

In the late 1970s three major events revolutionized these accounts. First, money market funds (see below) emerged as a major competitor to savings accounts. Next, banks lobbied for and won deregulation that allowed them to set interest rates (previously regulated) to compete with money markets. This exposed far more savers to the direct effects of these markets: rising rates during the inflation of the late '70s, and falling rates for the following 35 years. Finally, the automated teller machine (ATM) allowed depositors to deposit and withdraw cash at any time and without entering the branch.

Online banking has extended this convenience. A sensible home for some of your Envelope 1 is in a bank's savings account. Today you can transfer funds into your checking account online, so the distinction between savings and checking accounts is an anachronism. Not surprisingly, there is very little interest rate difference between these accounts either: each pays a few basis points, or none at all. The best rates are generally offered by banks that avoid the cost of a branch structure. You will probably find it desirable to hold these funds in a FDIC-insured account, since they are your core reserves and the source of all spending over the next one to two years. FDIC limits are currently $250,000 per account. This represents a temporary increase from the former limit of $100,000, enacted to forestall bank runs during the 2008 global financial crisis.

Savings accounts' mission is stability of principal, not growth. You will never brag to your friends at the neighborhood barbecue about your savings account's great returns.

Money Market Funds

Corporate and government borrowers take on short-term debt—as short as overnight, as long as 90 days—to manage their finances. For example, if they have sold a product on credit, they may borrow funds that will mature when the customer is expected to pay them. These short-term debt instruments, generally known as commercial paper, trade in a multitrillion dollar "money market." Your money market fund purchases bundles of such debt.

Money market funds take a little more risk than bank accounts, so they can offer marginally better interest rates. But because their rates are still infinitesimal, and typically well below the rate of price inflation, they are not suitable for long-term investing. When a stock fund manager "gets bearish" and "goes to cash," typically she is shifting some of her portfolio from stocks to money markets.

While money market funds have come to be viewed as indistinguishable from bank accounts, this is a misconception. Their return can rise and fall with capital markets. If the issuer of one of the instruments a fund holds runs into financial trouble, investors will dump the issuer's commercial paper, which will depress the prices of the money market fund's holdings. This happened in the fall of 2008 when the original money market fund Reserve Primary Fund "broke the buck"—the value of its assets fell below $1.00 per share. Because these funds are so widely used, the federal government extended FDIC-like guarantees over these funds to stop a budding run. But money market accounts are **not** FDIC-insured unless they are offered by an FDIC member bank.

Certificates of Deposit (CDs)

Within the confines of a bank, beyond savings accounts, you can sacrifice liquidity for return. The general idea is to loan your funds to the bank for a longer period than overnight, such as six months or two years. The bank offers you a higher rate to compensate you for tying up your funds for a longer period. These instruments are "certificates of deposit."

CDs are not completely illiquid. Typically it is possible to withdraw your funds before the maturity date, but at the cost of a penalty—commonly the loss of any interest earned. So how can you use CDs to pay ongoing expenses? Use the bond ladder approach.

Say that your bank offers CDs at 6-month, 12-month, 18-month, and 24-month maturities. You can split some of your Envelope 1 funds into one-fifth increments. Use four- fifths to buy one of each of the four maturities, and keep one-fifth in a savings account. Spend the funds in the savings account over the first sixth months. Then when the first CD matures, use its proceeds to replenish the savings account. As each six-month increment passes, use the newly maturing CDs' proceeds to replace expended cash. After 24 months it will be necessary to rebuild your Envelope 1 with proceeds from the sale of other Envelope 1 assets or assets in Envelopes 2 or 3. This is a micro-cosm within Envelope 1 of the broader multi-envelopes approach.

This may seem a bit cumbersome, but it takes advantage of FDIC member banks' security while your money is earning some interest.

Structured Certificates of Deposit (CDs)

Banks can also issue CDs without declaring an interest rate for the term of the CD. They can "structure" the CD by linking it to an index; using certain formulas, interest is credited each year based on changes in the reference index. These CDs are FDIC-insured and principal-protected if held until maturity. These CDs typically have a cap; for instance, a CD might be linked to the S&P 500 index annual point increases up to a cap of 4.5%. If the S&P 500 moves up by more than 4.5% in any given year the CD is only credited 4.5%. If the S&P 500 has a positive price movement between 0 and 4.5% the CD is credited whatever that positive percentage is. If the S&P 500 has a negative return the CD will have no interest credited, but it will not fall in value.

Short- and Intermediate-Term Bond Funds

Bond funds can be classified by the type of issuer they patronize (e.g., government or corporate), and by their geographic scope (domestic or international). One very important distinction relates to the bond's maturity. Commonly, funds can be classified as very short-term, short-term, medium-term, or long-term. The very shortest terms of less than 90 days are the money market funds described above.

Since Envelope 1 contains funds you will use within about five years, the right bond fund invests in bonds or bond funds with similar maturities and duration. In the current era of financial repression (artificially low interest rates) the smart investor will focus on lower duration bond funds with average maturities shorter than the actual time frame of their Envelope 1. These funds will have limited exposure to interest rate risk. As a result they will not fall nearly as far in value in a rising rate environment as long-term bond funds will. If rates rise by the time of maturity, the funds can be invested at higher rates.

Bond mutual funds achieve diversification. Active funds offer the prospect of exploiting interest rate changes, but with expenses of fees. Due to the prospect of rising rates in the future we prefer fully principal-protected investments for Envelope 1, and prefer the use of bond funds in Envelope 2.

Bond Ladders

In principle you can stagger the maturities of individual bonds to achieve a bond ladder like the CD ladder mentioned earlier. But markups on individual bonds are high, and it is difficult to diversify with limited funds. We recommend short- and intermediate-term bond funds.

CHAPTER 11

Traditional Options II

. . . .

Stocks and Stock Mutual Funds
(Growth and Inflation Hedging, Envelope 3)

This asset type is the one most familiar to smart investors. Stocks have long enjoyed the highest returns of any major asset class. Your portfolio is almost certainly heavily populated with stocks or stock mutual funds. Over long periods stock indexes have returned roughly 7% per year after inflation. In real purchasing power, on average, stocks have doubled every decade.

However, good returns come at the price of volatility, and volatility causes emotionally motivated mistakes the smart investor cannot afford. Stock indexes periodically make heart-stopping declines. In 2008-09, the S&P 500 fell by almost two-thirds. But they also recover, enough to produce the impressive average returns just cited. In fact, broad market indexes have rarely declined over any consecutive 10-year period, and never over 20 years. Investing in stocks is a bet on capitalism, which has an unrivaled historical track record.

As discussed in Chapter 3, conventional wisdom suggests investing in very low cost stock index funds (funds that mimic a stock index). These may charge one-tenth as much as actively managed funds, and indexes beat the after-expense returns of most active funds. In recent years more small investors have seen the wisdom of this approach and have been redeeming active funds and directing the proceeds into index funds.

A growing body of research suggests that there may be superior alternatives to the conventional index. Standard indexes hold stocks in proportion to their companies' market capitalization, known as "market cap." "Market cap" is a measure of a company's size based on its stock price. By definition such weighting concentrates in the most popular stocks and underweights the least popular. Implicitly, this is a momentum-based approach, emphasizing those stocks that have risen faster than peers. This is the opposite of a value approach that instead emphasizes overlooked stocks. A number of indexes have been created that weight stocks based on a more traditional value measure. This is termed "fundamental weighting" or "smart beta." Fundamentally-based appears to modestly outperform market cap-based indexes. They are becoming more common as research demonstrates their superiority.

This is a book about managing all of your assets as a *portfolio*. Understanding these basics is important even if you pay an advisor to handle the details. (Working with an advisor will be addressed in Chapter 24.) But we recognize that some readers would prefer a one-stop shop: a single firm or fund that can do all of this, putting your portfolio on autopilot.

Several different types of mutual funds have attempted this task. Balanced funds came first. Balanced funds hold both stocks and bonds, unlike most funds which hold only one or the other. Commonly balanced funds aim for an allocation of 50/50 stocks/ bonds, or 60/40. Many large institutions employ variants on this simple allocation. Balanced funds generally rebalance periodically, that is, sell one asset class when its proportion exceeds its target in order to buy the class that has fallen below its targeted portion. Sensible asset allocation that is updated through rebalancing is one of the most important things an investor can do to achieve satisfactory portfolio performance—and one often neglected. You could do far worse than a balanced fund for your Envelopes 2 and 3.

Note however, that balanced funds strive to maintain the same asset allocation over time. But *your* ideal allocation will change over time as you approach your retirement date. Target date funds emerged in the 1990s to address this need. In these funds the asset allocation evolves over time as the target date—the owner's planned retirement date—approaches. For instance, with a target date of 2030, the fund might be 70% in stocks in 2000, but only 40% in stocks by 2025. First-generation target date funds generally use this traditional glide path toward declining allocation in stocks. (Eventually we can expect to see inverse glide path target date funds.)

Target date funds became a common investment choice in many company 401(k) plans in the 2000s, and the default fund in some of them. As the field of behavioral finance (the study of how investors actually behave as opposed to how economists theorized they behaved) grew, financial researchers came to realize how few employees thought carefully about their asset allocation or periodically rebalanced. Since the "ideal" allocation for any investor depends on their investing horizon, the idea of a target date fund was born.

Where balanced and target date funds' asset allocations are rigid and preprogrammed, tactical asset allocation funds are the opposite. The fund's leadership sets boundary conditions (minima and maxima) for each asset class' portion, then managers choose an allocation within the permitted set based on current market conditions. This looks perilously close to timing markets—that is, moving in and out of an asset class based on short-term predictions. Tactical allocators would argue that rarely is any asset class ignored entirely (i.e., its target proportion is never set to zero). By the same token, the fund cannot overweight an asset class beyond its maximum weight. Many tactical funds do have a wide discretion to invest anywhere, and may have no minimum or maximums for certain asset classes.

In Chapters 4 and 5 we discussed the changing economic, political, and demographic environment into which the baby boomers will retire. We stated that the smart investor will have to contend with lower long-term returns from both stocks and bonds. In this new normal there is some indication that tactical mutual funds should be part of the smart investor's Envelope 3 holdings. A *tactical* mutual fund is one where the fund management team has a wide discretion in terms of security selection and asset allocation. By contrast, most mutual funds specialize in a specific asset class and/or style of investing. For instance, you can invest in a large cap growth fund—a fund that invests in large capitalization companies that are in their growth phase. Or you could invest in a small cap value fund which specializes in smaller capitalization companies that are currently out of favor by the investment public ("value" refers to the investor buying stocks offering a value because they are underpriced in the market compared to their intrinsic value). Then there are geographic funds like international stock funds or emerging markets bond funds.

A tactical fund can invest in virtually any asset class anywhere. These fund management teams can invest in stocks, bonds, commodities, currencies, derivatives, and so forth. They typically can invest anywhere in the world, and their prospectuses often permit them to not fully invest; in other words, they could move to cash during stressful periods in the capital markets. The term "asset allocation" is used because these funds typically have floors and ceilings of the portion of their portfolio permitted to be in a specific asset class. For example, a fund might be constrained to never have less than 80% of its assets in equities, and never more than 90%. Managers continuously change the allocation with these limits based on their view of relative asset values. Allocation targets may be specified in the prospectus of a tactical fund or may be entirely in the discretion of the fund's management team.

We have discovered a handful of these tactical funds that have substantially outperformed the S&P 500 index over the 14 years from January 2, 2000, to December 31, 2014. In nominal terms (i.e., not adjusted for inflation) the S&P 500 index's compound annual return in those years was 4.20% per year—that includes the strong bull market since March 2009. If we adjust the S&P 500's return for inflation, the annualized real return comes to only 1.91%! Typically your Envelope 3 investments will have a 10- to 15-year time horizon before you need to start accessing these funds. Much of Envelope 3 will have an even longer time horizon because only a portion will be used to refill Envelopes 1 and 2 at first. The goal of Envelope 3 is to outpace inflation. A run of the mill vanilla S&P 500 index fund would have done that for the 14-year period we've studied, although not by much. As we noted earlier the average retiree's personal inflation rate is probably going to be higher than the consumer price index. Moreover, the 2000 to 2014 period enjoyed historic low inflation. What if inflation becomes elevated in the future and the stock market's return over the next 14 years is near zero in real terms? That is why one of our suggestions to the smart investor is to broaden the investment vehicles used, including adding a healthy dose of tactical funds.

The reason tactical (also known as go-anywhere funds) have outperformed index funds over this period is because they tend to not be fully invested in stocks, and they have the ability to move to safe assets, resulting in lower losses during periods of stress than fully invested index funds. However, the smart investor has to understand these types of funds tend to underperform during strong bull markets, which was the case since 2009.

We are not taking a side in the longstanding debate between proponents of active vs. passive investing; i.e., selecting active mutual funds where the managers pick stocks they think will outperform the market versus investing in a passive index fund mirroring the market. During the accumulation phase you should heavily overweight index funds. When you get closer to retirement, or are retired, you should add more tactical funds with lower volatility to your mix.

We mentioned before that dividends are smoothers of volatility. Strong dividend-paying stocks or funds should be part of Envelope 3's mix. As the logic of the envelopes approach dictates the smart investor should focus on *income generation*, this is easier if dividends, interest, and capital gains distributions from Envelope 3 continuously pour into Envelope 1.

CHAPTER 12

Traditional Options III

· · · · · · · · · ·

Annuities
(Envelope 1 and Envelope 2)

Annuities are insurance contracts in which the insurance company invests your premium and pays it back to you in regular installments over an agreed upon time period. That period may be determined, such as 10 or 15 years, or indeterminate, such as your remaining life. Insurance companies pay out not in a lump sum at a distant, unknown date, but in a stream of payments that begin on a date of your choosing. As mentioned in earlier chapters there are many different types of annuities and the term is very broad and generic. For Envelope 1 the smart investor can choose from three types of annuities—single premium immediate annuities (SPIAs), fixed annuities, and fixed index annuities (FIAs).

Single Premium Immediate Annuities (SPIAs)

SPIAs are a bet with the insurance company: The longer you live, the more payments you receive. Annuitants (the persons receiving income) who live for a shorter time than the actuaries' predicted averages subsidize those who live longer. Of course, none of us knows our lifespan in advance. If you live longer than the life expectancy tables used by the insurance company you "win," since the insurance company has to continue to pay the promised income until you pass away. If you die before the life expectancy date used by the insurance company, the insurance company "wins" since they don't have to pay anymore.

There are a number of variations to a SPIA. You can select a contract (remember, an "annuity" is a contractual agreement between the investor and the insurance company) that allows for a "period certain." What this means is the insurance company will pay the income stream for a certain period regardless if you are alive or dead. Let's say the smart investor selects a SPIA with a 10-year period certain. The insurance company is now contractually obligated to pay the income stream for 10 years regardless. In other words, if the smart investor passes away after only two years of receiving income, the insurance company has to continue to pay the investor's beneficiaries for another eight years. However, if the investor is still alive at the end of 10 years the insurance company has to continue to pay the income stream for the remainder of the investor's life. Ten years is a floor, not a ceiling, under "period certain."

Of course, the annual payments for a period certain SPIA are lower than for a SPIA that only pays while you're alive. Why select a period certain SPIA? Because you are willing to give up a higher income in exchange for the certainty that your lump-sum payment (premium) won't disappear if you should unexpectedly die early in retirement.

Another variant of a SPIA is the joint contract, which will continue to pay until the surviving spouse passes away. This joint life SPIA will pay less income than a single life SPIA. There is also the SPIA for a "period only." This type, which is not commonly used, pays for only the period selected and then terminates. If you selected a period of only 10 years the insurance company pays for 10 years regardless if you are alive or dead and it terminates after 10 years regardless if you are alive. Ten years is the ceiling and the floor for payments under a period-only SPIA.

How to Use SPIAs

The amount of the payment is determined by four variables. There is the investor's age and sex, which are the primary determinates of life expectancy. Then there is the prevailing interest rate. The insurance company uses an internal rate of return (IRR) as part of the computation in determining the guaranteed income stream. This IRR is based on the prevailing interest rate environment at the time. Lastly, there is the *type* of SPIA selected. As we mentioned, the simple life-only SPIA will have a higher income amount, all other things being equal. Features like a joint-life, and period certain, will reduce the annual income stream.

Although the smart investor can consider whether she wants to add any of these features to hedge against early death, in Envelope 1 the main raison d'être for this investment vehicle is a longevity hedge. This portion of your money cannot be outlived. The secondary reason is to have current income from a source that is principal-protected. Regardless of what happens in the capital markets the annuity investor has transferred that risk to the insurance company. The income will continue to flow per the contract. Envelope 1 is all about stable and predictable income that is protected from market gyrations. Fluctuation or market risk is sequestered to the other envelopes, mainly Envelope 3.

Considerable research demonstrates that retirees whose income mainly comes from pension-like sources, including SPIAs, are happier and experience less stress than those who rely solely on assets.

Fixed Deferred Annuities

All "annuities" discussed below refer to "deferred annuities," i.e., annuities that have not commenced paying the investor an income. A fixed annuity is comparable to a bond or bank certificate of deposit. It is almost like an insurance company CD, without the FDIC insurance that a bank provides. The investor commits his money to a certain period, typically between four and seven years, at the conclusion of which the fixed annuity is no longer subject to a surrender penalty (comparable to a bond or CD maturity).

Where a bond can be sold at any given day in the open market before it matures, a fixed annuity has a surrender penalty for early liquidation, similar to a CD. This surrender schedule can be pretty hefty in the early years. When using a fixed annuity in Envelope 1 the smart investor should plan to have adequate liquidity to avoid being forced to liquidate the fixed annuity early. If your time frame for Envelope 1 is seven years then a fixed annuity with a four- or five-year term could work. Like a CD, the insurance company promises a fixed interest to be credited to the amount of money invested in the deferred fixed annuity. Often there is a minimum interest guarantee for the entire term, with the insurance company having the option to declare a new annual interest to be credited each year as long as it is above the contractual minimum. There are no internal fees or costs involved when investing in a fixed annuity, with the exception of the surrender penalty if you should ask for your money back before the end of the term.

While CDs are an important component of Envelopes 0 and 1, the advantage of a fixed annuity is that it typically offers a better interest credit than a comparable CD for the same term. Also, in a rising interest rate environment the annual interest reset feature will be beneficial. Unlike the typical CD most fixed annuities declare a new interest rate credit each year. There also is a tax advantage since the IRS classifies all annuities as tax-deferred vehicles when utilized outside of an individual retirement account. A smart investor with a high federal marginal tax bracket will benefit significantly from the interest credits not being taxed each year, leaving more in the fixed annuity contract to compound. Remember, when you own a CD at your local bank the interest credited to the CD is reportable income each year and taxed at your applicable income tax rate even if you don't withdraw it in that year. With a fixed annuity, the interest earnings are taxed only upon liquidation. The advantages of tax deferral are exponential—compounding over time—the longer the term of the fixed annuity.

Upon the end of the term you can surrender the annuity (since there is no surrender penalty anymore) and utilize the proceeds for income through the remainder of the Envelope 1 time period. Or, you can annuitize the fixed annuity, which means creating a single premium immediate annuity (SPIA) —giving the insurance company all the proceeds in exchange for a lifetime income payment. One tactical strategy we recommend to smart investors is to find an insurance company that offers an elevated internal rate of return once you annuitize a fixed annuity for a limited period, like only for five years. In a very low interest rate environment the smart investor can significantly outperform most short-term fixed investment instruments by using this strategy. An advisor can help you identify attractive offerings.

A fixed annuity fits very well in Envelope 1 but the smart investor could use a longer term fixed annuity for the first phase of Envelope 2 as well.

Fixed Index Annuities (FIA)

Like a fixed annuity, a fixed *index* annuity (FIA, also called an equity-linked annuity or equity index annuity) is a deferred annuity, where the investor defers taking income until sometime in the future. However, instead of the insurance company declaring an interest credit each year the interest is credited by using some reference index like the S&P 500, or the Dow Jones Industrial Average. There are many varieties of fixed index annuities which differ in complexity.

The main criticism against fixed index annuities revolves around some contracts' exceptionally long surrender periods and the fact that the true performance of these annuities doesn't mirror the index they are supposed to track.

We acknowledge the issue of extensive surrender periods should be a concern, and that the complexity of how interest is credited could create confusion. This does not mean these products should be excluded and there is a place for them in a well-diversified income-oriented retirement portfolio. We have heard many investors say, *"I don't invest in anything I don't understand."* This is commonly stated when they're discussing an investment vehicle like a fixed index annuity or other apparent esoteric investment products like a non-traded business development company (which we'll address in a later chapter). Most clients making this statement have investments in mutual funds and individual stocks. Investing is by nature complex. Does an investor really understand the intricacies of a major publicly traded corporation like General Electric, for instance, or the erstwhile Enron? Do investors really understand the complexities of how the long-term performance of stocks are influenced by inherent features of modern capitalism, like the instability and fragility of modern finance that manifested catastrophically in the 2008 financial crisis? We want to remind investors that "familiar" is not the same as "simple" or "easy to understand."

The point we're trying to make is that investing is complex and with the major economic and demographic trends discussed in earlier chapters, investors will need to shift their investing paradigms if they want to meet their retirement income goals. Some fixed index annuities should be part of this new investing paradigm. So let us explain the basic mechanics of a typical fixed index annuity (FIA).

Like a fixed annuity a FIA has a term; most contracts have terms between four and 10 years. An index is used by the insurance company to compute the interest credited to the contract. Some FIA contracts will allow the investor to select from two or more different indexes and a fixed account. The investor can allocate once a year among these indexes or fixed accounts. Let's say an investor can choose among the S&P 500, the Dow Jones Industrial Average, and a fixed account paying a fixed interest rate for the next 12 months. The investor could divide his money in the annuity in three equal pots, linking one-third to each of the two indexes and one-third to the fixed account. The one-third of the investment dollars linked to the fixed account will with certainty earn whatever the interest rate the insurance company has declared for the next 12 months. What the other two-thirds will earn depends on the performance of the two selected indexes. Virtually all FIAs track only the price movement of the offered indexes excluding dividends. Also, insurance companies "cap" the participation of the investor in the price movement of the index. These "cap rates" are declared every 12 months as well. Using our hypothetical FIA contract with two indexes and a fixed account, an insurance company can declare for the next 12 months that the fixed account will pay 1%, and the two equity indexes are capped at 4.5%. Let's say the S&P 500 over a 12-month period has an index return of 7% (i.e., the value of the index price increased by 7%) and the Dow Jones has an index return of 4%. The one-third of the investor's dollars linked to the S&P 500 index will be credited 4.5% because of the cap. The cap determines the maximum credit regardless of how well the S&P 500 performed. The other third of investment dollars linked to the Dow Jones will only get credited 4%, mirroring the actual performance of the Dow index since that performance was below the cap. In this hypothetical example the total interest credit for the entire contract over the 12-month period of time is 3.15% (assuming 34% of the investment dollars were linked to the fixed account and 33% each to the two indexes).

In a low interest rate environment a FIA is a competitive product suitable for Envelopes 1 and 2. It is complex, but it is principal-protected and has no internal fees, only the surrender charge. When the indexes' returns are negative the dollars allocated to the indexes earn zero percent: there is no participation in negative markets. Moreover, once an index had a negative year the investor in a FIA doesn't have to "make that up." The 12 months following the negative year start at whatever the index price point is, and if it is positive over the following 12 months the investor participates up to the cap. Let's look at a practical example.

On January 2, 2008, the S&P 500 index opening price was 1,467.97; it closed at 903.25 on December 31, 2008. This represented a price decline of 38.47%. If an investor linked all her FIA dollars to the S&P 500 during this period her interest credit would be 0% (full principal protection). If the investor kept her dollars allocated to the index through 2009 her interest would have been 4.5% (assuming a hypothetical cap of 4.5%). Thus, the FIA investor would have had a total return of 4.5% through 2008 and 2009. Nothing to write home about, but how does that compare to an investor invested in an S&P 500 index fund? Ignoring index fund fees, a fund that mirrored the exact total return of the S&P 500 through 2008 and 2009 would have had a negative total return of –20.20%, reflecting the S&P 500's –37.22% return in 2008 followed by a positive total return 27.11% in 2009. At the end of 2009 the investor had not yet made up for the losses of 2008. Let's be clear, though, a FIA is not a growth investment. Because of the caps it will never be able to compare to the index's total return over time. It is a conservative fixed investment with principal protection. Therefore it is appropriate for Envelopes 1 and 2.

The smart investor can do better using contracts with "spreads" or "margins." They differ from the capped indexing approach in that "spread" contracts declare that the investor will receive the index's price performance as an interest credit minus an upfront spread of, say, 3%. In other words, the investor won't receive the reference index's first 3% return (the "spread") but the investor is not capped on the upside. Granted, most "spread" products don't use traditional equity indexes like the S&P 500 or the Dow Jones. They use blended indexes that include bonds. Here the insurance company manages its risk through the upfront spread and the fact that the reference index is not 100% equities but an asset allocated diversified reference index containing stocks and bonds.

If a diversified stock and bond reference index has a loss over one year the investor has a zero percent credit. Assuming a 3% spread or margin, if the reference index has a 7% return the investor is credited 4% (7% minus the 3% spread).

Just like fixed annuities, the FIA investor can take all the proceeds from the contract at the end of the term to help meet income needs or annuitize the contract for a lifetime income stream.

Remember, a fixed index annuity is a CD-like investment. It is too often positioned as a stock market investment with principal protection. It will never perform in line with the stock market when stock prices rise. Returning to our analogy earlier, comparing annuities to vehicles that transport people, fixed annuities and fixed index annuities are like bicycles. But the following type of annuity, a variable annuity with a living benefit rider, is more like a plane. This is how big the differences can be among these annuities.

Variable Annuity (VA) with a Living Benefit Rider

Another type of annuity that fits well in Envelope 2 (and even Envelope 3) is a *variable annuity with a living benefit rider*. We like to refer to a *living benefit* rider as a *protected income base*. This annuity differs significantly from the other types discussed so far. The term "variable" refers to the fact that the value of the annuity will fluctuate—the contract value can vary on a daily basis. As explained earlier, annuities are contractual agreements where an insurance company agrees to pay an income stream for a certain time period—typically for life. While the previous three types of annuities we discussed have principal protection, a variable annuity's principal fluctuates with movements in the capital markets. There are many varieties of variable annuities, with significant differences in how they function. We will try to provide a general description of how these sometimes complicated instruments operate. Also, some variable annuities don't have so-called living benefit riders—an added feature that protects a stream of income while the investor is alive without the investor having to annuitize. ("Annuitize" is where the investor loses control of the principal by giving it to the insurance company and receiving regular payments.)

A "living benefit rider" is a very unique feature of receiving income from an annuity contract by establishing a protected income base. The investor maintains income control over the under-lying investment funds, and the income stream can be canceled or suspended at any time. The underlying investments are always available as a lump-sum withdrawal. By contrast, with a SPIA, once you hand the money over to the insurance company you cannot take it back, nor do you have access to the principal anymore—you only receive the income stream.

Let's start with a description of a basic variable annuity. It is a contract that states that the value on which your income stream will be based is determined by the performance of your selection of sub-accounts. "Sub-accounts" are essentially mutual funds that the insurance company offers to the investors to select from within their insurance contract. This aspect is what makes the annuity vari-able—the investor's money is invested in the capital markets through "mutual funds" and will fluctuate or vary with the performance of those funds. Most sub-accounts within variable annuities are actually clones of retail mutual funds available to investors outside of annu-ities. For explanatory purposes we'll refer to sub-accounts as funds.

The menu of funds offered within a variable annuity differs significantly and it is critical for the smart investor to evaluate the available funds when considering a variable annuity contract as an investment. In each contract there is usually a wide range of fund choices to select from. The most common choices are asset alloca-tion funds: funds that invest in securities of different asset classes like stocks, bonds, international stocks, and emerging market secu-rities. Each asset allocation fund is structured to meet certain risk tolerance levels. There are aggressive funds, growth-oriented funds, moderate funds, and conservative funds. The more aggressive the asset allocation fund the greater the stock market or equity exposure as a percentage of assets in the fund.

Most variable annuity contracts also have traditional mutual fund choices as sub-accounts, like large cap growth funds or small cap value funds. Some contracts include as options alternative type funds like managed futures funds or real estate investment trust funds. And some contracts include tactical funds as part of their menu. As discussed earlier the difference between a tactical fund and an asset allocation fund has to do with the discretion of the fund management team. An asset allocation fund has strict rules on how fund assets are allocated amongst different classes of investments based on the risk profile of the fund as well as on modern portfolio theory calculations. A tactical fund, on the other hand, allows the management team much wider discretion to allocate the capital of the fund based on the management team's reading of capital market and economic trends.

In deciding which insurance company's variable annuity product to use the smart investor should always focus on those contracts with the most fund choices, especially those contracts that offer choices of tactical, alternative, and asset class specific funds, not just asset allocation funds. However, fund choices are not the only factor to consider.

Once money is placed in a variable annuity contract the investor controls how the "premium" (investment amount) is distributed among the funds, and the investor can move among funds at no extra cost. The funds the investor selects will fluctuate (vary) in line with how the underlying securities selected by her fund managers perform. Over time the cumulative performance of the investor's basket of funds, which the investor can change at any time, determines the "contract value," which is the combined value of the funds at any given time. If the funds have fallen in value, the contract value may be lower than the original investment.

Let's say an investor invests $100,000 into a basic variable annuity contract selecting four funds, and seven years later the cumulative value of the four funds (the contract value) is $150,000. The investor then has the option of either withdrawing the $150,000 and rein-vesting it somewhere else, or annuitizing the $150,000 to start a SPIA that will pay the investor a pension-like income. In some years some of the funds selected will have positive returns and in other years some will have negative returns, with the net cumulative perfor-mance over time determining the contract value. The investor takes the risk of the cumulative value being less than the original invest-ment due to poor fund and market performance. Her $100,000 may only be worth, say, $90,000 when she wants to start taking income. There is thus principal risk associated with a variable annuity that is avoided with SPIAs, fixed annuities, and FIAs.

Why use a variable annuity contract as opposed to just directly investing in a basket of mutual funds? What is the advantage of the contract and its fees if the investor is carrying all the risk? When variable annuities were created the basic contracts offered two advantageous features. First, variable annuities have death benefits. The typical basic death benefit feature of the contract states that if the investor passes away and the contract value is lower than the original investment or principal the beneficiaries will receive a death benefit amount equal to the original investment. Therefore, benefi-ciaries are protected against poor fund performance if the contract holder should die. The second feature is tax deferral. All deferred annuity contracts (contracts with income that hasn't started yet) — fixed annuities, fixed index annuities, and variable annuities—held outside of retirement accounts or employer-sponsored retirement plans still retain the benefit of tax deferral. Investors won't have to pay capital gains, dividend, or interest income taxes while the money is in the annuity contract. Many investors use variable annuity prod-ucts as a way to invest in mutual funds with their taxable money to avoid paying gains, dividend, and interest income taxes each year. The IRS sees annuities primarily as retirement vehicles. Tax deferral becomes exponentially more advantageous the longer the investor leaves the money in the annuity contract.

Annuities and Taxes

But annuities' principal protected death benefit and tax deferral come at a price. (In the world of investing everything has tradeoffs.) Since the IRS sees these products as retirement vehicles they have certain tax features like retirement accounts and plans. In exchange for the tax deferral you have to deal with a premature withdrawal tax penalty of 10% if you take money out of an annuity contract before age 59 ½—just like an IRA. Furthermore, if you "surrender" the annuity contract (withdraw the contract value as a lump sum), any gains are treated as ordinary income and taxed at the investor's marginal income tax bracket. Money invested directly in mutual funds, not indirectly through annuity contracts, are taxed at a different (and most of the time lower) tax rate for dividends and capital gains.

These are important disadvantages. The issue of premature withdrawals is essentially a non-issue for smart investors using this product as part of the envelopes approach we propose, since the smart investor will make sure she is older than 59½ before accessing these contracts for income. If an investor needs the proceeds from, say, a fixed annuity in Envelope 1 before age 59½ then the smart investor will either use a contract with a longer term as part of Envelope 2, or not use an annuity contract at all. This tax penalty does not apply to SPIAs. Variable annuities we propose for use in Envelope 2. Only a minority of investors are privileged enough to retire so early that they will access Envelope 2 before age 59½.

Another reason the premature withdrawal issue is no big deal when using our envelope approach is because we prefer to use variable annuities in Individual Retirement Accounts. The tax character of annuities in IRAs are the same as for annuities held outside of IRAs. Money distributed from IRAs are taxed as ordinary income just like annuity contracts. All other investment-related taxes inside IRAs are avoided as long as the money stays in the IRA. The same holds true for annuity contracts.

The tax treatment of annuity contract assets is a very important factor requiring planning. Let's return to the hypothetical investor who invested $100,000 in a variable annuity contract using four funds. Most years these funds will have capital gains distributions, dividends, or interest income which inside a variable annuity contract are just reinvested in the funds. Also, if our investor switches from one fund to another and the fund being "sold" or switched out of had a gain, that gain is now also reinvested in the new fund. While all of this activity takes place within the variable annuity contract, no 1099 tax form is generated at the end of each calendar year and the investor owes no taxes. This is the same tax treatment IRA and other retirement arrangement assets receive. If the same four funds were held outside of the variable annuity contracts a 1099 form would be issued by each fund and the investor would have to pay taxes each year. Remember, for this explanation we assume our investor invested taxable money, not money in IRAs or other retirement plans. This tax treatment looks like a great advantage, right?

Well, there is a downside. Continuing with our example, assume after seven years the investor has a contract value of $150,000 and decides to surrender the contract, so the investor now has a gain of $50,000. This gain is taxed at the investor's marginal income tax bracket. If the investor held the same four funds outside of the variable annuity contract and sold them with a $50,000 gain that gain is considered a long-term capital gain and taxed at the applicable capital gains tax rate, which in most instances is a lower rate than the investor's marginal income tax bracket.

Another downside is that if the investor died right before surrendering the contract the beneficiaries would receive a $150,000 lump-sum death benefit. Because of the unique tax character of annuity contracts the beneficiaries will incur **income** (*not* capital gains) taxes on the $50,000 gain. If the investor held the funds outside of the annuity contract and died with a $50,000 unrealized gain in the funds (meaning she died while her money was still invested in the funds) her beneficiaries would receive a step-up in cost basis. In other words, if they sell the funds after the investor's death their cost-basis is now $150,000 and they only pay taxes at the capital gains tax rate on any gains above $150,000.

This is a huge deal; annuities are not ideal vehicles to die with, from a beneficiary's perspective. Money held in a retirement account is treated the same for tax purposes as an annuity contract upon death, so dying with a variable annuity held inside a retirement account doesn't change how taxes are paid by the IRA beneficiaries. The beneficiaries of a retirement account do not receive a step-up in cost basis because in a retirement account no taxes have been paid, so the cost basis is zero. A Roth-IRA is the exception since only after-tax money can be invested in Roths. This is another reason we prefer to hold variable annuity contracts inside IRAs. Conventional wisdom for a long time was to use variable annuities outside of retirement accounts to receive tax deferral, but we believe if variable annuities are used for the purpose of adding the protected income base feature guaranteeing lifetime income, a retirement account is often a better vehicle to hold them.

Living Benefit Riders

There are occasions when variable annuity contracts could and should be used with non-retirement assets to obtain tax deferral, specifically when used primarily for the death benefit. But when you add the living benefit rider (feature) the smart investor should try and use retirement assets to invest in the variable annuity contract.

So what is this living benefit rider we keep referencing? Under the basic mechanics of a typical variable annuity contract, an investor places money in an annuity contract among a menu of fund choices. The value of the contract will fluctuate with the performance of the selected funds. Insurance companies offer a feature (or "rider" in insurance-speak) that can be added to the contract for an extra cost. This feature offers insurance protection against market loss if the contract holder commits to take an income stream over time. By adding this feature to your variable annuity contract the contract has a second value—the protected income base. The "contract value" is the value of the investor's selected funds which fluctuates on a daily basis. The protected income base does not fluctuate. When the smart investor invests in the contract the protected income base is equal to the original amount invested; returning to our earlier example, $100,000. Most living benefit riders have two ways of increasing. First, typically every 12 months, if the contract value is higher than the previous 12 months' value the income base steps up or increases permanently in line with the value of the underlying funds. Second, if the contract value doesn't increase, or it declines over a 12-month period, then the protected income base will increase by a fixed percentage as stipulated in the contract.

Example of Living Benefit Rider During Withdrawals

We know this seems very complicated, but in fact, all investments are complex and convoluted. It may not seem that way for some investments, but if you dig deeper they all are multifaceted. Back to our hypothetical investor who invested $100,000 in a variable annuity contract with a living benefit rider. She picked her four funds and she intends to only access the annuity for income beginning seven years in the future. On Day 1 of the contract her account value is $100,000 ($25,000 in each fund), and her protected income base is $100,000. Her contract stipulates that the protected income base will increase by 5% per year or the increase in the contract value, whichever is greater. So if her funds grow by 5% or less the protected income base will step up by at least 5%, but if her funds increase in value by more than 5% the contract value will cause the protected income base to step up to equal the contract value.

Assuming our investor's funds have a combined net increase of 15% the first year of the contract, on Day 1 of the second year of the contract the contract value would be $115,000 and the protected income base would be $115,000. In year two the total value of the four funds only increased by $2,000, resulting in a contract value of $117,000. Because this increase was less than 5% of $115,000, the protected income base will now step up to $120,750 (because 5% of $115,000 is $5,750).

On Day 1 of the third year of the contract our investor's contract value is $117,000 and her protected income base is $120,750. The difference between these two values is that the contract value can be withdrawn as a lump sum (minus any surrender charges) and the protected income base is available only as a stream of annuity payments. Assume that year three is bad for our investor. Her funds drop in value due to a bear market, dragging her contract value down from $117,000 to $105,000. However, her protected income base increased by the mandatory 5% from $120,750 to $126,788. Remember, for the smart investor it is all about the income, stupid!! It is income that matters. If the smart investor has done proper planning there will ample assets elsewhere to meet liquidity or emergency needs. Therefore, the focus with the variable annuity is to increase the protected income base. This is why we believe this product is an indispensable part of most smart investors' repertoire.

In year 4 of the contract things are improving in the market and the contract value goes up to $120,000 as a new bull market surges and our investor's four funds post stellar performances. Even though her funds posted a 14.29% increase the contract value did not surpass the protected income base of $126,788. Per the contractual living benefit feature the protected income base now increases to $133,127 (the contractual 5% increase).

In the fifth year the bull market continues to surge and our investor's four funds post a 20% positive return, pushing the contract value up from $120,000 to $144,000! Since this return is more than 5% of the previous protected income base of $133,127 the protected income base now steps up to equal the contract value of $144,000.

Figure 12-1 Increasing Value of Protected Income
vs. Fluctuating Account Value

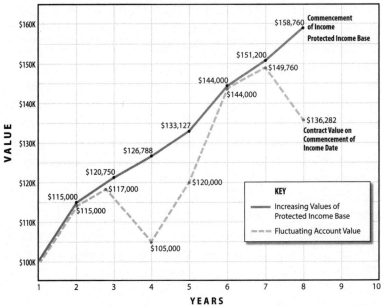

In the sixth year the bull market cools down a bit and the funds only post a 4% return, increasing the contract value from $144,000 to $149,760. The protected income base, on the other hand, increases by the contractual 5% to $151,200.

In the seventh year—the last year before our smart investor wants to commence with the income from the annuity—the markets take an unexpected turn for the worse and her funds have a loss of 9% for the year. This decreases the contract value from $149,760 to $136,282. The protected income base, though, increases to $158,760.

At the beginning of year eight our smart investor wants to start taking her income per her envelopes plan. Most living benefit riders stipulate that the investor can take a percentage of the protected income base each year based on the investor's age at the time income commences. This is called "age banding." Most variable annuities with living benefit riders allow a 4.5% to 5% withdrawal from the protected income base if the investor is between the ages of 65 and 70, with a 1% increase of the permitted income withdrawal rate between 70 and 75, and another 1% increase if the investor is older than 75. The withdrawal rate is determined by the age you *start* taking withdrawals. These income streams are protected for life. Don't confuse the withdrawal rate, typically 5% when you're 65 to 75, with the 5% guaranteed increase of the protected income base before you begin taking withdrawals. The withdrawal rate is the percentage of the income base permitted to be withdrawn as income. The guaranteed increase or step-up refers to the minimum percentage *increase* the income base will go up with each year. It is also important to remind the investor that once income starts, you can still be fully invested in risky funds because your income base is insured.

Let's assume our smart investor is age 65 when she wants to commence income and let's assume her contract allows for a 5% withdrawal rate at that age. That means if her protected income base is $158,760 then she is entitled to withdraw $7,938 per year for the rest of her life. With most variable annuity contracts with living benefit riders the fixed percentage increase (in our example the 5% minimum increase of the protected income base) will end once income commences. There is no more guaranteed increase of the income base once our investor starts her lifetime income stream. That being said, the income base can still increase if the value of the funds grows and pushes up the contract value (minus withdrawals) beyond the previous high-water mark of the protected income base.

Let's continue with our hypothetical example above. It's year eight of the contract and the two values of our investor's contract are $136,282 for the contract value (the value of the four mutual funds) and $158,760 for the protected income base. Remember, the investor can decide to walk away with a lump sum of $136,282 or she can take a lifetime income of the protected income base of $7,938 per year. Our smart investor decides to start taking the income. Immediately upon withdrawal of the income her contract value is reduced by the amount of the withdrawal and is now $128,344 ($136,282 – $7,938 = $128,344). The protected income base is not reduced because these types of contracts guarantee the income stream for life and the base determines the amount of the income—in this case 5% of the base or $7,938. It's important to remember that in the aforementioned example the lifetime income stream of $7,938 per year represents a 5.82% distribution ratio of the contract value ($7,938 is 5% of the funds' value of $136,282). It will be very difficult for the contract value to sustain this distribution rate over the long term—remember our discussion that sustainable withdrawal rates are probably below 4%—but our smart investor is not worried. She is using the envelopes approach and has ample liquidity in Envelopes 0 and 1. She is committed to continue taking the lifetime income as part of her overall income plan. Moreover, she continues to maintain control over the underlying investments after income commenced. She still controls how the money is invested and allocated among the menu of funds available inside the contract. If circumstances change she always has the option of walking away with the contract value as her lump sum. This means the contract is not technically "annuitized" as in a single premium immediate annuity. "Annuitization" means the insurance company controls your money and you only receive an income stream. In this case our smart investor continues to control the contract value and always has the option to walk away with the contract value as a lump-sum withdrawal.

Continuing our example above, through year eight our investor's funds have a positive return of 12%, increasing the contract value from $128,344 to $143,745. The protected income base remains at $158,760 since the 5% fixed percentage increase is no longer available after income commences. The only way for the income base to increase hereafter is if the contract value surpasses it.

At the beginning of year nine our smart investor withdraws her protected lifetime income of $7,938 per year, reducing her contract value from $143,745 to $135,807. The markets surge in the ninth year and her funds post a 20% return, increasing her contract value from $135,807 to $162,968. Since this is higher than her protected income base it steps up her base from $158,760 to $162,968. This, of course, resets the lifetime income amount because 5% of $162,967 is $8,148 per year. Her annual lifetime income has now increased from $7,938 to $8,148 *permanently*. It can never decrease. Even if the contract value goes to zero the insurance company has to continue to pay the $8,148 each year for the life of our smart investor.

We'll end our hypothetical example in year 10. Let's assume there is another major financial crisis comparable to 2008. Let's assume our smart investor's funds lose 40%, resulting in her contract value plummeting from $162,968 to $92,892. This sounds severe, but that happened during the financial crisis. Our smart investor is not worried because she will continue to receive $8,148 annually for the rest of her life. This income stream now represents an impossible to sustain distribution rate of 8.77% if she had her money invested directly in the four funds. If she did not use the variable annuity with the living benefit feature she would not be able to withdraw $8,148 as part of her annual income. She would have had to reduce this income in years the market declined; moreover, if a calamity like the financial crisis occurred, similar to our hypothetical year 10, she would have had to drastically reduce her income.

Table 12-1 shows how the variable annuity with the protected income base could work in the hypothetical example above:

Explanatory Notes: The second column titled *Value of "Mutual Funds" (Contract Value)*, refers to the fluctuating value of the underlying investment funds. The column titled *% Market Return* refers to the net percentage change (negative in parenthesis) of the underlying investment funds for that year. The *Protected Income Base* refers to the contractual guaranteed amount from which the investor can take income. The *Protected Income Base* starts off being the investor's original investment (premium) and can only increase. It increases by the market's percentage return, or 5%, whichever is greater. The *Lifetime Annual Income* column refers to the yearly amount of income the investor can take based on the *Protected Income Base*. In our example

Table 12-1 Variable Annuity with Protected Income Base

Years	Value of "Mutual Funds" (Contract Value)	% Market Return	Protected Income Base	Lifetime Annual Income End of Year
Day 1, Yr 1	$100,000	15% for year 1	$115,000	
Day 1, Yr 2	$115,000	1.74% for year 2	$120,750	
Day 1, Yr 3	$117,000	(10.26%) for year 3	$126,788	
Day 1, Yr 4	$105,000	14.29% for year 4	$133,127	
Day 1, Yr 5	$120,000	20% for year 5	$144,000	
Day 1, Yr 6	$144,000	4% for year 6	$151,200	
Day 1, Yr 7	$149,760	(9%) for year 7	$158,760	
Day 1, Yr 8	$136,282	12% for year 8	$158,760	$7,938
Day 1, Yr 9	$143,745	20% for year 9	$162,968	$7,938
Day 1, Yr 10	$162,968	(40%) for year 10	$162,968	$8,148
Day 1, Yr 11	$92,892			$8,148

the formula to determine the lifetime income is 5% of the *Protected Income Base*. Once income commences the only way the *Protected Income Base* can increase is if the investment funds grow, after the income withdrawal, to surpass the *Protected Income Base*, as in year nine. In year 10 there was a financial crisis resulting in a 40% decline of the underlying investment funds. The contract value on Day 1 of year 11 is $92,891. Our example doesn't go further, but the annual lifetime income remains at $8,148 until the contract value grows to surpass $162,967, the previous high-water mark of the *Protected Income Base*. If the contract value never surpasses the *Protected Income Base* amount due to the income stream of $8,148 representing an 8.77% distribution rate of the contract value, the annual lifetime income remains $8,148 for life. When the $92,891 is spent down to zero because the funds' growth was not able to overcome the distribution rate, the income continues for the life of the investor.

When selecting variable annuities with living benefit riders that protect an income base the smart investors should focus on contracts that allow them as much freedom to choose the underlying investment funds. It's not just a matter of how many menu choices of funds a contract has, but how free you are to move among these funds. Many contracts restrict what percentage can be invested in riskier asset classes like emerging markets. Since you're paying the insurance company a fee for the income base protection, you should be allowed maximum freedom. Select those contracts with the fewest restrictions.

Income base features or living benefit riders are not cheap. Over time there will be a significant compounded fee drag on the performance of the underlying value of the investment funds, potentially impacting the step-ups. We think the protection is worth the cost for a portion of your retirement portfolio.

Variable Annuity with a Return of Principal Rider

This type of deferred annuity is not commonly used, but it could be useful in Envelope 2. Being a variable annuity the contract has underlying "mutual funds" you can chose from. Instead of adding a feature protecting your income base in the future, you can select a feature that protects the actual lump-sum value of your investments at a future date. Many contracts have a term of 10 years stating that your original investment amount is guaranteed against loss. If the value of the investment funds dropped below your original investment the insurance company makes up the difference. You're entitled to receive your entire original investment back as a lump sum. This type of contract doesn't have an income base, only a contract value (value of the mutual funds). It guarantees the original investment against market declines. The value of this type of annuity contract is the principal protection it provides and hedging against sequence of returns risk—as discussed earlier, this is the risk of negative returns shortly before you need to take income.

Table 12-2 Comparing Annuities

Type	Purpose	Envelope
Single Premium Immediate Annuity (SPIA)	Lifetime Income	1
Deferred Fixed Annuity	Fixed interest like a CD	1 or 2
Deferred Fixed Index Annuity (FIA)	Interest based on a reference index	1 or 2
Variable Annuity with Protected Income Base	Lifetime income with market exposure	2 or 3
Variable Annuity with Return of Principal	Insurance against loss for lump sum	2

For illustrative purposes, a hypothetical smart investor following the envelopes approach will have Envelope 2 filled with very conservative and moderate risk investments like bond funds. Our smart investor decides to use a variable annuity with a return of principal feature over 10 years in Envelope 2. Our investor's Envelope 1 is of course filled with safe investments which will provide cash for his income needs for seven years. His Envelope 2 investments will need to start covering his inflation-adjusted income needs beginning in year eight through year 15. Envelope 3 will take care of year 16 and beyond. By year 10 when our smart investor needs to use the funds invested in the return of principal annuity he won't have to be concerned with market losses, because he is guaranteed to receive at least his principal back. Granted, he wouldn't have had any growth on that portion of his portfolio; however, retirement is all about income generation, therefore a zero percent return is infinitely better than having a loss right before you need to use the money for income.

Why Are Annuities a Polarizing Product?

Criticism of annuities revolve around three issues: fees, complexity, and control. The subject can be polarizing. One view, heavily promoted by a prominent investment manager, emphasizes the very significant fees associated with variable annuities. If you've visited financial websites online you might have seen the ubiquitous ads saying, *"I hate annuities and you should too."* This opinion is overly simplistic to the point of being misleading.

Fees

Of the annuities we discussed only variable annuities have internal fees. Yes, these fees are steep. A variable annuity with a living benefit rider protecting an income base can have all-inclusive fees of around 3.5% to 4%. Insurance companies typically pay insurance agents and financial advisors generous commissions. Sales can easily be overdone. The fees inside variable annuities are high, but we don't think they are excessive. Actually, one of the pioneers in variable annuity research, Moshe Milevsky, in a 2006 paper entitled "Financial Valuation of Guaranteed Minimum Withdrawal Benefits," argues that variable annuities with living benefit riders are actually underpriced. In our estimation the fees charged by insurance companies for variable annuities with protected income bases are not excessive. The investor is shifting market and longevity risk entirely onto the insurance company. If you live long and the markets perform poorly you will probably spend down your contract value. Every check you receive after that is the insurance company's money. Since you can take more risk with the funds inside a variable annuity with a protected income base you will in all likelihood outperform investing the same money outside of a variable annuity, where you have no insurance protection.

There is a likelihood that an investor in a variable annuity with a protected income base guarantee could end up only receiving back his own money because the underlying investment funds' performance was adequate to pay the income stream. That's comparable to paying your homeowners' insurance for 60 years and never having your house burn down. All those premiums could have been invested, and with compounding over time could be a significant amount of money the insurance company gets to keep. The compounded fee will drag down the investment value; however, the smart investor will be aware of the type of environment he is retiring into as we've discussed earlier in the book, and there is no way to know what capital market returns will be in the future. Will returns be adequate to sustain your desired income stream? Given the macroeconomic environment discussed in Chapter 4, capital market returns will be lower than historical averages for some time. Coupled with increases in life expectancy and medical advances, it is imperative that the smart investor has some longevity hedges.

All Annuities Are Not Alike

Single premium immediate annuities, fixed annuities, and fixed index annuities do not have internal fees like variable annuities. It is disingenuous to lump all annuities together. As we indicated, the term is so generic it's not only impractical, but actually misleading to refer to "annuities" as a single type of product. The only thing all the types of annuities have in common is that the investor has the option to annuitize them—handing over the value of the contracts to the insurance company in exchange for a stream of income. Too much of the criticism is very simplistic and it's not adequately nuanced.

Annuities can be complex with a lot of moving parts, but that doesn't make them "bad" investments. The way Social Security benefits are calculated and the different choices in receiving benefits (like file and suspend, restricted applications, spousal benefits, etc.) can be just as complex, or even more complex, as some types of annuities, yet the vast majority of Americans consider Social Security as a "good" investment. Furthermore, not all annuities are complex. A SPIA is like Social Security or a company pension plan—in exchange for a lump sum you receive a stream of income. A fixed annuity is like a CD. With the exception of a higher surrender charge or penalty and no FDIC insurance, there is really no difference between a CD and a fixed annuity.

The criticism of loss of control has to do with liquidity. Remember, all investments have tradeoffs. If you want to have a stream of lifetime income you have to trade away liquidity, or access to the principal in the case of a SPIA, or access to the protected income base of a variable annuity. If you want to have a better interest rate than a fully accessible savings account you invest in a CD, a fixed annuity, or a fixed index annuity. In all three cases you have to commit to a maturity date or incur a penalty when you liquidate early.

There is a growing body of empirical research published by peer-reviewed academic journals showing the value of annuities to retirees. It is an indispensable part of the smart investor's repertoire. In the resources section we provide a list of these peer-reviewed articles. Virtually all academic research is in favor of utilizing certain types of annuities. But it can't be denied that some types of annuities have excessive surrender periods and penalties. Annuities can be overused and certain annuities are used incorrectly or sold to retirees too old to fully benefit from certain features.

Annuities in Your Retirement Portfolio

Opposite is Figure 12-2; it illustrates a concept designed by Professor Milevsky to show what he refers to as three product silos for your retirement nest egg. He recommends you look at the lump-sum values of your Social Security or pensions and add them to the total value of your retirement nest egg. He recommends approximately one-third of your retirement portfolio to be allocated for long-term growth using mutual funds or managed accounts, with a focus on equity investments. This is similar to our Envelope 3. Of your total portfolio one-third should be focused on providing lifetime income. Social Security, pensions, and single premium immediate annuities provide your longevity protection—a critical issue in ensuring your portfolio lasts as long as you do. This silo is similar to our Envelope 1. Milevsky's "Sequence of Returns" protection silo refers to variable annuities with protected income bases. When markets perform advantageously you can lock-in the market gains as part of your protected income base, allowing this silo to boost your growth

Figure 12-2 Three Product Silos for Your Retirement Nest Egg

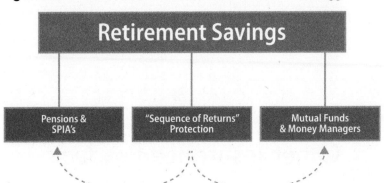

investments to help offset inflation and rising costs over time. When markets perform poorly you have a protected income base that will provide lifetime income, ensuring you won't outlive your income.

In sum, we believe that annuities have great features, but we acknowledge high fees of variable annuities. We recommend annuitizing only enough to top off other pension-like sources to meet fixed expenses. Also, the way we generally recommend using fixed annuities and fixed index annuities is not part of this general calculation since you won't take annuity income from these two vehicles. Remember, just because the term "annuity" is in the name of a product doesn't make it an annuity, i.e., a stream of income. From our perspective, annuities are indispensable to the smart investor's retirement income plan. These investments are not intrinsically "good" or "bad"—it all depends on how the smart investor utilizes them.

CHAPTER 13

Other Insurance Products
. . . .
Secondary Market Annuities and Viaticals (Envelope 2 and Envelope 3)

Insurance products have great virtues, but life circumstances may change. The purchaser may find that the product no longer fits her needs. A common example: The family breadwinner's life insurance policy may no longer be necessary once the kids have become financially independent.

Just like the market for used cars and lived-in houses, there are secondary markets for some insurance products. Secondary market annuities (SMAs) allow the original purchaser of the annuity to tap its value by selling it to a secondary purchaser. The annuity will still pay out on its original schedule (a fixed term, or lifetime), but it now pays the new owner. Lifetime SMAs sometimes are bundled with a life insurance policy on the original owner so that the purchaser can be assured of a return if the annuitant dies earlier than expected.

Owners of life insurance with cash value may likewise wish to liberate that value by selling the policy. A morbid but common instance is of a terminally ill policyholder who needs to pay medical expenses. These transactions are termed "viatical" contracts. The new owner receives a lump sum—the life insurance payout—when the insured dies. Individual investors can invest in these secondary insurance products by purchasing an individual insurance contract, or invest in a pool of contracts.

For both SMAs and viaticals, brokerage and other fees can be expensive. This market has emerged in the past few years, so regulation is spotty. Most financial advisors cannot sell these products since they are not publicly regulated investment products. These products are only sold by specialists in this field who are not obligated to look at an investor's overall portfolio to determine suitability. Proceed with great caution.

CHAPTER 14

Dividend Stocks and Dividend Mutual Funds
· · · · · · · · · ·
(Envelope 3)

Dividend-paying stocks and funds are important components of a portfolio aiming to generate a sustainable income stream. *Total return* comprises changes in the price of a stock, plus any dividends the company pays to shareholders. The company's board determines the quarterly dividend paid. The generosity of dividends is captured by the *payout ratio*—the fraction of total profits paid out. Because some profits must be reinvested to maintain company growth, payout ratios above a threshold, like 70% of profits, are not considered sustainable unless the company is in a mature industry that does not need much reinvestment. By contrast, new firms or new industries often pay no dividends at all: Those funds can be used more productively fueling growth.

In round numbers stocks' historic 7% annual real total return has come less from capital gains (price changes) than from dividends. A stock's dividend yield captures its dividends divided by its share price. The dividend yield for a broad market index currently is around 2%, below historic norms. Yields tend to shrink in strong markets (because stock prices rise far faster than dividends); conversely, yields rise in a down market.

Income investors are typically those whose investing horizon is relatively short—like smart investors in their decumulation stage. Dividend stocks mainly provide income, with some prospective capital gain. Considerable research has demonstrated that dividend stocks also have useful defensive properties: the dividend cushions the stock's fall in down markets. Over long periods of time dividends generate as much as two-thirds of a stock index's total return.

Common dividend stocks are those in mature industries that cannot profitably reinvest all of their earnings. Dividends are a way of returning value to shareholders instead of keeping it locked within a slow-growing company. Increasing numbers of firms also return cash by repurchasing shares, which make outstanding shares more valuable as company ownership is spread among fewer shareholders.

Even better are companies that consistently *increase* either their share repurchases or their dividends. While you are accumulating it can be profitable to reinvest these proceeds to buy more stock, so your holdings compound. Many companies offer dividend reinvestment programs, or DRIPs, sometimes offering a discounted price for the purchased shares, which further accelerates accumulation.

Companies that return increasing amounts of cash to shareholders, either through dividends or repurchase, are very nearly perfect investments. They are relatively safe (for stocks), because the consistent payment record is only possible if the company has consistent, predictable earnings. This cash flow can help maintain demand for the stock even in a down market, limiting downside. And the commitment to return cash to shareholders disciplines company management: it is harder to be tempted by foolish acquisitions, and harder to fabricate earnings when cash must be generated every quarter.

In the new normal of slow growth in the developed world, many more industries will seem mature, and will need to attract investors through dividends rather than capital gains. A number of stock screens related to dividends exist, such as S&P's Dividend Achievers and Dividend Aristocrats. Most mutual fund families have one or more dividend-oriented stock funds.

The smart investor constructing a retirement portfolio will want to overweight (emphasize) dividend-paying stock funds, stocks, and money managers in Envelope 3. There are many tactical variations in managing the envelopes, especially when it comes to moving assets among the envelopes as Envelope 1 gets close to being spent down. The approach we propose in Chapter 6 is to let all the dividends from investments in Envelope 3 pour into Envelope 1—except in such cases when the prices of the investments in Envelope 3 drops precipitously during bear markets. Then it makes sense to reinvest the dividends to buy cheaper shares of the funds or stocks.

CHAPTER 15

Pass-Through Alternative Investments

· · · · · · · · · ·

REITs, MLPs, and BDCs
(Envelope 3)

Not surprisingly, as the new normal has revived interest in dividends, the popularity has only grown of a type of business whose central purpose is dividends.

The standard business form is the "C corp"—an entity (corporation) for which its owners assume only very limited liability, usually limited to the value of their investment. Owners employ managers who tend their interests. Managers are overseen by boards of directors, which represent owners. Corporations are liable for taxes on their earnings. So corporate owners—stockholders—experience double taxation: first at the corporate level, later on the income they earn from their stock ownership.

"Trusts" have long existed as legal vehicles that can pool investors' resources to own shares in C corporations. Many of the robber barons of the late 19th century organized their holdings into trusts, so U.S. antimonopoly law began with the Sherman *Antitrust* Act of 1890. Generally these "pass-through entities" (so called because tax liability passes through the firm to its owners) must be organized as partnerships. Common partnerships are services firms that need to retain little in the way of working or growth capital, such as law or accounting firms, so nearly all profits are paid to partners.

REITs: Real Estate Investment Trusts

Starting in 1960, Congress legalized other business forms that avoid corporate taxation. The real estate industry came first, lobbying for the creation of real estate investment trusts (REITs). As noted in an earlier chapter, REITs hold groups of income-producing (rent-earning) properties. To maintain their corporate tax-exempt status, REITs and other pass-through entities must distribute at least 90% of their net earnings to shareholders. This permits yields two to four times higher than most C corps offer.

Because REITs avoid taxation on the corporate level most of their dividends are not "qualified" to be taxed at the lower dividend tax rate. Most REIT dividends are taxed as ordinary income at the investor's marginal tax rate (therefore some of the yield advantage of REITs are lost through taxation). This is similar to how interest from bonds, CDs, and savings accounts is taxed. Also, REIT distributions are often classified as both dividends and a partial return of investors' capital. The latter occurs when the REIT distributes more than its net income, mainly because it can deduct depreciation of their real estate. This, of course, reduces the cost basis for investors. The portion of the dividend that is classified as a return of capital is not taxed at either the dividend tax rate or the investor's marginal tax rate.

REITs are extremely dependent on debt markets for growth capital, since they cannot retain earnings for growth. REITs are highly interest rate-sensitive, since they must borrow to buy new properties. Publicly traded REITs could also raise capital through

Figure 15-1 REITs: Real Estate Investment Trusts

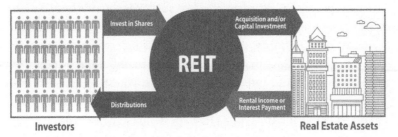

issuing more shares in the public market but this would dilute current shareholders' value.

Types of REITs

There are three basic types of REITs. Equity REITs own real estate and collect the rental and lease income from their portfolio of properties. Mortgage REITs own loans or mortgages and collect the mortgage payments. Finally, hybrid REITs own both mortgages and real property. Most REITs also specialize in a certain segment of the real estate market industry. There are residential REITs, office and industrial REITs, health care REITs, self-storage REITs, and hotel and resort REITs.

Companies are increasingly reconfiguring themselves as REITs as a financial engineering move. The northwest company Weyerhauser did this in the early 2010s. A number of companies have spun their real estate holdings off as REITs and now lease back from the spinoff REIT the buildings formerly owned by the company. At this writing Sears Holdings has proposed spinning the real estate occupied by about 300 stores into a REIT, from which the company will lease. Several firms have sold off and rented back their headquarters buildings.

Pass-through entities like REITs generally suffer from several disadvantages. Happily, these are less significant to the smart investor.

Pass-through entities are organized as partnerships. The general partner typically has nearly unchecked authority: boards have far less scope of governance than those of C corps. This will not matter if you expect to be a minority shareholder. Nevertheless, restricting your search to those entities that have a track record of putting owners first will help protect your interests. For example, you should favor those whose management owns a significant fraction of total shares. This is a good principle for any type of firm, pass-through or C corp.

Because pass-through entities distribute almost all of their earnings, they are poor choices for growth investors. But the general drift of your portfolio will be away from growth as your retirement progresses (although you will always need some growth-oriented assets in Envelope 3). So pass-through entities are a very appropriate part of Envelope 3.

MLPs: Master Limited Partnerships

Close behind the real estate industry in lobbying muscle is the energy industry. It secured congressional agreement for a REIT-like corporate form for energy firms, known as master limited partnerships (MLPs). While MLPs were originally intended for energy infrastructure, as their tax advantages have become apparent, they are now being used for a host of real property investments, including in rail cars and chemical plants. MLPs must generate 90% of their income from natural resources-related activities, including exploration, storage, transportation, and production. Unlike a REIT an MLP only has to distribute income as set forth in the partnership agreement. To be competitive with other MLPs, income distributions are relatively high. There is no legal requirement for the level of distributions an MLP must make. By custom distributions are tiered, providing an incentive for the general partner to distribute more income to the limited partners.

Typically, the general partner controls management and operations of the MLP through a 2% equity stake in the MLP. The limited

Figure 15-2 Typical MLP Ownership Structure

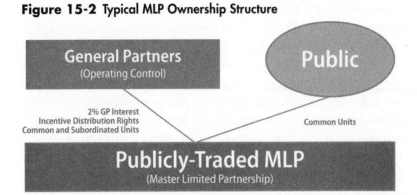

partners own the remainder of the MLP's units. MLPs typically distribute all of their cash on hand on a quarterly basis, excluding some reserves as determined by the general partner. The general partner has first priority to receive cash distributions up to an established minimum referred to as the minimum quarterly distribution amount (MQD). Cash in excess of the MQD is then distributed on a pro rata basis among the general partner and the limited partners.

MLP agreements also have incentive distribution rights whereby the general partner is rewarded for distributions that surpass specified target levels. As the general partner increases cash distributions the general partner receives an increasing portion of the incremental cash distributed. These increasing percentages are the "tiers" of the MLP.

The income distributed from MLPs has huge tax advantages. Like REITs they are not taxable on the corporate level, being classified as a pass-through entity. MLPs are allowed to designate virtually all of their income distributions as "return of capital," resulting in no income or dividend taxes having to be paid on their distributions. However, the "return of capital" classification causes the cost basis of the investor to decrease. Compared to REIT distributions, the overwhelming majority of a MLPs distribution is classified as a return of capital due to exceptionally high percentages of depreciation on energy properties and equipment allowed by the tax code. The portion of the distribution that is not classified as a return of capital is taxed as ordinary income, like REITs.

Although these are substantial advantages for the MLP investor, the tax reporting can be complicated. Investors won't receive 1099s but rather K-1 statements, which is a partnership income tax form. Different states also have different reporting requirements. To minimize tax hassles, but more importantly to achieve diversification, the smart investor should consider investing in MLPs through a mutual fund or a closed-end fund. Mutual funds deal with the K-1 requirements and issue the easier 1099 tax reporting form.

The original energy-related MLPs have been classified as "upstream" (energy exploration and production) and "downstream" (refining and distribution). Recent history has demonstrated some MLPs can also thrive under declining energy prices. "Midstream" pipeline MLPs, for example, earn revenues based on the volume of oil or gas they transport. Lower energy prices will stimulate demand, pulling more through the pipeline system.

BDCs: Business Development Companies

Business Development Companies (BDCs) are closed-end investment companies; in other words, technically closed-end mutual funds. These funds were created by the Small Business Investment Incentive Act of 1980, with a dual purpose to provide capital to private companies, and to create a vehicle for individual investors to invest in them. There are fewer than 4,000 publicly traded companies that are actively traded. The overwhelming majority of individual investors invest in the stocks or bonds of publicly traded companies, directly or indirectly through mutual funds and other investment funds. Although most of America's largest corporations are among these 4,000 companies, the vast majority of companies in the U.S. are private. There are literally millions of private businesses in the U.S. from mom-and-pop diners, to Cargill and Koch Industries.

Figure 15-3 BDC: Business Development Companies

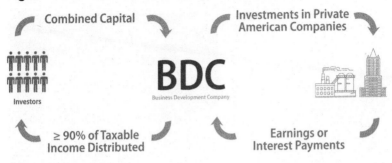

Until it went public in 2012 Facebook was one of the nation's largest private companies. If you exclude very small private business, there are 200,000 companies that fall into the so-called "middle-market," companies with revenues between $10 million and $1 billion per year. This is the segment where BDCs invest.

Investments in private companies until 1980 had always been the mainstay of the ultra-wealthy, and institutional investors like pension funds, insurance companies, and private equity firms. Even with the creation of BDCs the private company space is still dominated by private equity firms and institutional investors. We believe, however, that BDCs, offer opportunities to the smart investor. From a diversification standpoint, why should you be restricted to 4,000 actively traded stocks? The smart investor should want to broaden her portfolio into the private sphere, and BDCs offer the ideal vehicle to do so.

For a fund to be classified as a BDC and avoid taxation on the corporate level, like other pass-through entities, it must invest at least 70% of its assets in private U.S. companies or thinly traded public U.S. companies. Also, the fund has to distribute 90% of its net income to its shareholders. Figure 15-3 is a schematic explaining how a BDC functions.

Individual investors purchase the shares of a BDC, which pools the capital of investors and then makes investments in private

Figure 15-4 Corporate Capital Structure

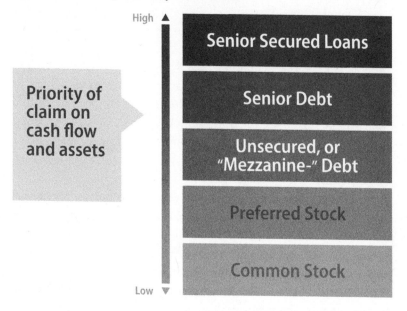

American companies. The earnings or interest payments made by these companies to the BDC are distributed as dividends to the individual investors.

Similar to REITs there are three types of BDCs: namely, debt BDCs, equity BDCs, and hybrid BDCs. Debt BDCs invest primarily in the debt of private companies. We prefer debt BDCs that focus on senior secured debt at the top of a company's capital structure.

A company's capital structure has several levels representing priority of claims on the cash flow and assets of the company; in other words, it determines who gets paid first. At the top are loans secured by the borrowing company's collateral. These are the most senior loans since if the company fails to make a payment on the secured loan the lender can take the company's assets, like equipment, vehicles, inventory, real estate, and accounts receivable. "Senior debt" means loans that are contractually placed above other loans for repayment, but these loans are not secured by the company's assets or collateral. Below the two levels of senior debt are different classes of debt that are neither senior nor secured. This means if a company goes into bankruptcy the senior secured lenders are paid first; if there is not enough cash to pay them, they can take the company's assets and sell it off to get back the money they lent the company. Only if there is enough assets to pay the senior secured lenders, next in line to be repaid are the other senior lenders. After all the senior lenders are paid, and the bankrupt company has assets left, then the unsecured lenders are paid. Debt BDCs lend into the top three levels of a company's capital structure.

Debt BDCs own two types of loans, those that are purchased in the secondary loan market and loans the BDC or its sub-advisor *originate*, where they directly negotiate the terms with the borrowing company.

Equity BDCs are not lenders to private companies but rather they become co-owners of the companies. They focus on the bottom portion of the companies' capital structure since they take equity positions in the companies where they invest. Where debt BDCs are focused on generating regular income for their shareholders, equity BDCs, on the other hand, are focused on capital appreciation. The exit strategy of an equity BDC is to sell its stake in the private company for a profit, and distribute that capital gain to its shareholders. Often the triggering event is when the company issues publicly traded stock (an initial public offering or IPO). Equity BDCs are considered riskier than debt BDCs because equity holders rarely recoup their investments if a company goes bankrupt and is liquidated.

Hybrid BDCs lend money to private companies *and* they buy ownership stakes (equity) in private companies. Some hybrid BDCs are mostly debt BDCs that may sometimes take small equity positions in companies that they lend to through warrants or other types of equity, known as "equity kickers." This allows them to enjoy some upside.

CHAPTER 16

Traded vs. Nontraded?

. . . .

(Envelope 3)

The Liquid-Traded Pricing Mechanism

Pass-through entities are appropriate for the smart investor's growth Envelope 3. The smart investor can hold them directly by buying shares in these pass-through companies, or indirectly through using mutual funds, ETFs, or separate account money managers. The issue we want to turn to now, though, is somewhat controversial and much misunderstood. In the previous chapter we recommended three main pass-through entities—MPLs, REITs, and BDCs. MLPs can only be invested in through buying their shares on a stock exchange, or through ETFs and mutual funds that do so. REITs and BDCs can be bought either in the "traded" markets or the "nontraded" markets. This is an important distinction the smart investor needs to understand.

Publicly traded stocks change hands on stock exchanges all over the world. Buyers and sellers meet on these exchanges (elec-tronically through the brokerage firms they use) and buy or sell ownership shares of companies. At any given moment the price of an ownership share (called stocks or equity) is determined by a myriad of factors. The key determinant is supply and demand—if there are more buyers than sellers on an exchange at any given time the price of a stock will go up; conversely, if there are more sellers than buyers, the price will decline. During market hours, prices will fall or rise until all buyers and sellers are paired. Every night when we watch the news and learn the Dow is up 50 points it means that for the 30 companies making up the Dow Jones Industrial Average (which represent the largest, most well-known and sought-after U.S. stocks) there were more buyers than sellers. On that day prices of the Dow 30 had to increase until enough owners of Dow stocks were enticed to sell their shares to the buyers out there, who bid those prices up to become the new owners of those shares. If, the following day, the news reported the Dow was down 50 points, it means there were more sellers than buyers. The prices of the Dow companies decreases until the sellers enticed enough buyers at prices they were willing to pay.

These are important concepts to understand for many reasons. Starting with the most obvious, if you open your investment statements at the end of the month and they show the total value of your 401(k) declined by "X" amount of dollars, what does that mean? The most common reaction is, "Oh, I lost money this month!" One of the authors has experienced this reaction from his spouse many times. The author's reply is, "It doesn't mean you lost money; it means on the last business day of the month there were more sellers than buyers, and that's why the price of your mutual funds was lower. You didn't lose anything, honey, because you didn't sell anything. You only 'lost' money if you sold at that lower price. Since you didn't sell, it only reflects a snapshot of prices in time. You only 'lost' money on paper." This explanation typically elicits, "Oh, that makes sense"… until the next month's statement shows another decline.

Liquid = Emotion-Driven

People are emotional; if they see lower prices for extended periods of time (which we call market corrections or bear markets) people start to fear that these prices are permanent, leading them to sell in panic. At this point they actually lose money, since they sold their investments at lower prices than they bought them. At any point in time prices don't necessarily reflect the true intrinsic value of the companies. They only reflect the reality that on that given day, or period of time, there were more people wanting to sell their stocks than buyers willing to buy.

Stocks and bonds that are traded will exchange hands based on this dynamic of daily matching buyers to sellers, known as "mark to market." "Liquid"-meaning sellers can liquidate their investments at any given day in the market. This liquidity in the traded markets is important, giving investors' peace of mind, knowing they can sell their stocks, bonds, or mutual funds whenever they want.

Not all assets are priced in liquid-traded markets. Many times when we look at our investment statements, and we see dollar value declines month over month, we forget about this important fact. For many Americans their biggest single asset is their home. Houses do not trade on liquid exchanges like stocks. Houses are offered for sale directly to buyers. If we had the same pricing mechanism for a house that we have for a stock then houses would be priced at zero most of the time. What? How can a house be priced at zero most of the time? Well, if no one knocks on your door on Tuesday and offers you a price to buy your house then your house should be priced $0 on Tuesday ... if you followed the pricing mechanism of liquid-traded markets. The same is true for your car, for that matter, or for your television set. These assets are therefore not liquid—they can't be liquidated at will.

The point we're trying to make at this stage is although the majority of individual investors will buy and own stocks, bonds, and mutual funds traded in public markets with prices determined by the liquid-traded pricing mechanism, this is not the only way to buy and own shares. Like your house, you can own illiquid assets, and you can't apply the liquid-traded pricing mechanism to such assets. Your house is not worth zero if someone doesn't knock on your door offering to buy the house on Tuesday, or any day for that matter. That's ridiculous, right?

A Range of Pricing Mechanisms

There are different pricing mechanisms for products and assets within the capitalist system. Each pricing mechanism has its advantages and disadvantages. The liquid-traded pricing mechanism, based on the principal of mark to market, has the very important advantage of being liquid. If you own Apple shares you can sell them and get your cash on any trading day knowing exactly the price being offered. The disadvantage of this type of market and pricing mechanism is the potential unnerving influence it has on investors' emotions. The liquid-traded pricing mechanism causes two emotions that could drive markets up or down to prices entirely unrelated to the investment's intrinsic value. These two emotions are fear and greed.

During the technology boom of the late 1990s, we saw technology stocks being bid up to dizzying levels. People were paying massively inflated prices for stocks of tech companies that had no earnings. This buying frenzy was driven by greed. People observed the liquid prices rising to ever increasing levels. Not wanting to lose out on all the "wealth" their neighbors were accumulating while these liquid prices kept on going up and up, many people were drawn into the market as buyers. The prices people were prepared to pay for tech stocks were fundamentally, profoundly, illogically, and stupidly unrelated to the real intrinsic value of these companies.

Eventually, people started realizing that the prices were far removed from the fundamentals, and selling commenced. This selling was reflected daily through the liquid-traded pricing mechanism, and like a light switch flipping off, fear and panic ensued, leading to prices dropping precipitously. The tech bubble burst, causing trillions of dollars of paper wealth to be destroyed.

The tech boom and bust are a stark reminder where the liquid-traded pricing mechanism produced prices entirely disconnected from the intrinsic value of companies. Another example is during the global financial crisis of 2008. The S&P 500 index, which follows the prices of the 500 biggest publicly traded U.S. companies, fell a dizzying 55% from its peak. Again, this was a dramatic example of fear driving prices downward. Can you really make the argument on March 9, 2009, when the S&P 500 index was at its lowest point, that these 500 companies, which include the likes of Apple, Microsoft, Exon, GE, etc., were worth only half their October 2007 value, before the commencement of the crisis?

The liquid-traded pricing mechanism very often produces price swings only tenuously moored to reality. The smart investor should understand this. The reason most individual investors underperform stock indexes is because of emotions. And there is nothing like the liquid-traded pricing mechanism that can provoke people's emotions.

De Facto Illiquidity

This brings us to another point about the traded markets and liquidity. Although the traded markets are liquid, price swings can lead to *de facto* illiquidity. Let's say you're a retired investor owning stocks of excellent and profitable companies. As the stock market rose from 2003 through 2007, you have increased your allocation to stocks because every month you opened your statement you saw the dollar prices ever increasing: you were making money; you were accumulating wealth. In reality, only by selling at those elevated prices would you actually make money, which you did occasionally to meet your income needs. You had some cash and some bonds which you used to supplement your retirement income, but more and more of your portfolio consisted of stocks, some of which you liquidated every year for retirement income. Overall, though, the fraction of your portfolio in stocks rose.

Then 2008 happens. The prices of your stocks start to plummet. To meet your retirement income needs you use your cash savings, then sell your bonds. You're disciplined and have a long-term view: you're not going to sell your stocks at these prices. But, by the beginning of 2009, you have to start living on less income. You have to spend less, because you used all of your cash and bonds, and now all you have are stocks, and they're not generating enough dividends to meet your income needs. Although your stock portfolio is fully *liquid*—on any given day you can sell stocks and have the cash you need for income—the depressed prices of these stocks force you to act like it is *illiquid* since you don't want to sell at these prices. Your "liquid" stock portfolio has become *de facto* illiquid!

But, what if you don't have the luxury to wait? What if you really need the income, or you have a medical emergency that you need to cover? Then you are forced to sell at depressed prices, locking in losses you can never make up, since the money is spent and can't be reinvested. This is why we profess the envelopes approach, of course!

What if you panic? What if you can't stand to see the drop in value and fear it will continue and "never" turn around? Then you sell, incur the losses, keep the money in cash, and are so burnt by the process, you will be slow to reinvest the money, miss most of the turnaround, condemning yourself to a permanently smaller retirement portfolio. Again, this underscores the wisdom of the envelopes approach.

The liquid-traded pricing mechanism is important, and by extension, having liquidity is crucial for the smart investor. But, there is also value in having some of your investments outside of the traded (emotional) markets. During times of panic or exuberance, the traded markets may start to *correlate*, meaning that all stocks start going down due to fear, or up during times of greed. When investments correlate it defeats diversification. Isn't the aim of diversification to have investments that each act differently during periods of stress and euphoria? The goal of diversification is to have investments that perform "independently." When some investment prices decline for whatever reason you want other investments to increase in price; we call this inverse correlation. Or when some investment prices decline precipitously, you want other investment prices to decline less, or remain more stable—this is low correlation.

Low-correlated diversification is the main reason to have investment vehicles outside of the traded markets. It helps the smart investor with the unavoidable emotions of liquid fluctuations. If it helps the investor avoid panic selling, it can help the smart investor's portfolio's total return over time. Think about the use of a variable annuity with a protected income base discussed in an earlier chapter. The value of the mutual funds in the variable annuity is determined by the liquid-traded markets. When those markets suffer psychologically induced price declines, the existence of the protected income base could provide peace of mind for the investor since the protected income base won't decline in line with its traded mutual funds. The income base is protected, because it is insured by the insurance company, and it is a nontraded value, not based on the gyrations of the liquid-traded markets. This same logic holds for the nontraded versions of two of the pass-through entities discussed in the previous chapter, REITs and BDCs.

Traded and Nontraded REITs

Many investors are familiar with *traded* REITs and BDCs, because their shares trade on stock exchanges like any other publicly traded stock. But others can be "nontraded" or "non-listed." This is an important distinction because the risk characteristics, liquidity, and performance of REITs and BDCs are influenced whether they are "traded" or "non-listed."

The majority of individual investors will utilize *publicly* registered REITs as their investment vehicle to gain real estate exposure. There also are *private* REITs, which are not registered with the Securities and Exchange Commission (SEC), and are not traded on any exchange. Like any private company, private REITs that intend to later become public (i.e., offer their shares to the investment public at large) will have to go through a rigorous filing process to register their shares with the SEC. As public companies they have many more disclosure and reporting requirements than private companies, to ensure transparency to individual investors.

The majority of public REITs offer their shares on a national stock exchange. Some public REITs, though, offer their shares directly to the public. REITs that do this are referred to as "nontraded" REITs. Sometimes they are referred to as "private" REITs, but this is incorrect since a nontraded REIT has to register as a public company, just like its traded cousin, and is therefore not truly private. The only major difference between a traded and a nontraded REIT is how shares exchange hands (although this leads to other important differences). Publicly traded REIT shares are priced through the liquid-traded pricing mechanism, whereas public nontraded REIT shares are priced using certain valuation methods to appraise the underlying real estate, dividing the net value of the underlying real estate by the number of shares available.

When a private REIT decides to go public, it goes through an underwriting process led by an investment bank that results in an initial public offering (IPO). "Going public" is not cheap. Substantial legal and investment banking fees are involved to list shares on an exchange. The price at which a publicly traded REIT starts trading is already inflated by the underwriting spread the investment banks charge, and the REIT's net earnings reflect other fees incurred in the IPO. From this point forward a traded REIT is like any other traded stock in the sense that one investor buys the shares of a particular REIT from another investor at prices set daily in liquid-traded markets. In other words, all trades after the IPO are in the secondary market (the IPO was the primary market). The REIT received cash from listing its shares in the initial public offering. Subsequent selling of shares on an exchange doesn't bring new money to the REIT, it only exchanges ownership of the shares.

A nontraded REIT, on the other hand, does not go through the process of listing its shares, but it does go through the SEC registration process, and must adhere to the same requirements as other publicly registered companies. Nontraded REITs offer their shares to the public through the broker-dealer community and their affiliated financial advisors. When a nontraded REIT opens, it offers shares to the public at a nominal price per share. On Day 1 of a nontraded REIT's existence the REIT has no properties yet: it has not raised capital yet to buy them. It declares by prospectus the real estate investment strategy it will follow. For instance, it might be a commercial office REIT, or a health care REIT buying health care-related properties. As the nontraded REIT raises cash through the sale of shares, it deploys the cash by buying the intended properties, passing through net income from rents to its investors. There has been some criticism of the fees and commissions associated with nontraded REITs in raising capital, and there are currently regulatory actions to address how they are disclosed. We feel the fees are somewhat excessive, but not to the extent that we discourage the smart investor from nontraded REITs in the long-term Envelope 3.

During this offering period, which could last for a couple of years, the nontraded REIT is "open." After some time the nontraded REIT closes to new investors. During its closed period the nontraded REIT manages its portfolio of real estate just like a traded REIT. However, with a traded REIT an investor can always sell his shares on an exchange at the current traded share price. Under the liquid-traded pricing mechanism this share price can be either more or less than the net value of the underlying real estate (called the *net asset value*). Shareholders in a nontraded REIT have no exchange to sell their share, and can only sell it back to the REIT company during specified redemption periods. At least once a year a nontraded REIT uses some type of valuation process to determine the value of the underlying real estate, which determines the share price. Because of the different pricing mechanisms used by traded and nontraded REITs the prices act differently even though a traded or nontraded REIT might own very similar real estate portfolios. Because nontraded REITs do not have their shares listed on an exchange it removes most of the liquid pricing psychology (fear and greed) discussed above. The desire of investors on any given day to buy or sell the shares of a REIT does not directly affect its share price. That is based more directly on the net value of the underlying real estate. (By net value we mean the total value of the entire portfolio of real estate owned by the REIT minus the debt of the REIT.) Nontraded REIT share prices are never priced at premiums or discounts to their net asset value, whereas traded REITs are almost never traded at exactly the net asset value of their underlying real estate, trading at either a premium or discount, due in part to the psychological factors we earlier discussed.

An Illustration

Here is a hypothetical example showing the way a REIT trade can increase or decrease the volatility in a portfolio. A smart investor invests a portion of his Envelope 3 money in two REITs—*ABC Realty* (a traded REIT), and *XYZ Properties* (a nontraded REIT). At the time of purchase of the shares of ABC Realty, interest rates are very low. Typically, during times of low interest rates, the demand for REITs is higher since their comparatively high dividends attract investors searching for yield. So ABC Realty shares trade at a premium to the net asset value of the company's portfolio of properties. In other words, imagine ABC Realty owns office buildings all over the country, and at their most recent appraisal the net value of these buildings is determined to be $10 billion. If ABC Realty had 100 million shares outstanding trading on the New York Stock Exchange and the price per share was $100, then the share price is trading at the net asset value: the share price exactly reflects the underlying value of the buildings. However, because interest rates in the country are very low, with a 10-year U.S. government bond paying 2%, the share price of ABC Realty will be bid up due to investor demand for the attractive 4% dividend the company is paying. Remember,

REITs have to pass through 90% of their net income to investors. The rents of the office buildings of ABC Realty (net of expenses) are paid out as dividends to the shareholders. Shareholders are paying $110 per share on the New York Stock Exchange for ABC Realty's shares when our smart investor makes his purchase. So our smart investor is paying a 10% premium over the value of the office buildings.

Our smart investor also buys shares of XYZ Properties, a nontraded REIT, that's been selling shares to the public through financial advisors for a little over a year. XYZ Properties owns industrial warehouses worth $1 billion and its shares are offered at a public offering price of $10.50 per share. This price includes a capital raising fee (load) of, say, 12%, which represents the fees and commissions paid out by the REIT to distribute the shares through the broker-dealer industry. This means the underlying value of the industrial warehouses based on the most recent appraisal methodology was $9.24. Our smart investor is paying a 12% premium, in the form of a load, but the remainder of the price is directly related to the net value of XYZ Properties' underlying warehouses.

Let's assume interest rates continue to move lower and the stock market is doing well, resulting in virtually all stocks going up in price. ABC Realty might trade at $115 per share (15% higher than its net asset value). In this interest rate environment XYZ Properties' offering price won't increase: it will remain at $10.50—the net value of its underlying real estate plus the offering load. Assume that a year later interest rates start rising. Now other yield-type investments like bonds become more attractive vis-à-vis ABC Realty. Through the liquid-traded pricing mechanism ABC Realty's share price declines to $108. Assuming the nontraded XYZ Properties haven't performed another appraisal, XYZ Properties' offering price remains stable at $10.50, with our smart investor's share value being $9.24.

This example illustrates how there often is more volatility in the share price of the traded REIT than the nontraded REIT. Taking the hypothetical example further, a year later the global economy shows signs of slowing down. Investors de-risk by selling stocks and the stock market starts to decline. A market correction is in full swing. ABC Realty's share price drops to $98 per share. XYZ Properties performed an appraisal and determined its industrial warehouses had only a 2% increase in value. Although the global economy is slowing down its industrial warehouses are still being leased and there continues to be a demand for warehouse space, resulting in a repricing of its shares to $9.42 (the previous share price of $9.24 × 1.02).

At this stage you might argue that it's not a big difference in volatility between the two REITs. You are correct, until fear sets in. Say that the economy goes into a recession, and the stock market moves into bear territory. ABC Realty's share prices decline by 25% from $98 to $73.50. The nontraded XYZ Properties, using its chosen appraisal method, experiences a decrease in the net value of its warehouses; in other words, if it sold those warehouses in the commercial real estate market it would probably get 5% less for the warehouses compared to a year ago. This is due to increased vacancies in its warehouses due to reduced use by companies affected by the recession. Our smart investor who bought the shares at the original offering price of $10.50 now faces a share price of $8.95 ($9.42 × .95).

In this scenario the nontraded REIT ends up being far less volatile because the psychology of the liquid-traded pricing mechanism of the stock market isn't operative. The traded REIT price declined by 36% from $115 to $73.50. The nontraded REIT price declined only 15%. In this example our smart investor will start reinvesting the dividends of both REITs in his Envelope 3 to buy more shares at depressed prices, undeterred by the temporary price decline, having certainty of his income from safe Envelope 1. But our smart investor is still only human. When ABC Realty's share prices decline further to $60 per share he starts feeling uncomfortable. Although, XYZ Properties' share price has also declined further to say $8.40, the smaller percentage decline of the nontraded REIT prices serve as an important emotional stabilizer for our smart investor. Due to fear, he might have reacted impulsively but for the stability offered by the less volatile nontraded XYZ Properties in his portfolio.

This example is one of the primary reasons we recommend using nontraded REITs. We want to be clear, though, this is not to say that nontraded REITs will always have less volatility, nor are we predicting their total return will be better than traded REITs. The key point we're trying to make is that nontraded REITs *might* react differently during times of stress since their prices are related to their net asset value more than a traded REIT, where the price is determined by the liquid-traded pricing mechanism, and is therefore less directly related to the net asset value of the underlying real estate.

The other advantages of a nontraded REIT during the REIT's open phase stem from the availability of cash. When a traded REIT listed its shares on an exchange during the REIT's initial public offering (IPO) it raised substantial cash. But after the IPO the only way a traded REIT can obtain money to purchase new real estate is by selling current properties or using debt. At these times a traded REIT is at a disadvantage compared to nontraded REITs. Nontraded REITs during their open phase have a constant inflow of new investor capital they can deploy. Of course, nontraded REITs will also use debt, but during their open phase they always have cash to buy properties. This could be an important advantage at times when real estate prices are depressed. Full cash offers or predominantly cash offers will increase the probability of the offer being accepted, especially if it is not contingent on the sale of another piece of property. (This is also true for your house.) So nontraded REITs can exploit real estate market declines more readily. This advantage could enhance the total return of nontraded REITs.

Regulatory Changes

As of this writing important regulatory changes are occurring in the pricing, regular valuation, and reported share prices of nontraded REITs. However, the basic premise of our argument remains unchanged. Traded REITs could have more volatility because of the emotional liquid-traded pricing mechanism. Nontraded REITs will continue to have share prices more directly related to the net value of the underlying real estate. See our website http://www.7secrets-retirement.com/ for more information on these regulatory changes and their implications.

Nontraded Business Development Companies

Many of the same dynamics are at play when it comes to nontraded business development companies (BDCs). Similar options exist for a smart investor when it comes to investing in private middle market companies. The wealthy smart investor can invest directly in a private company through a private placement, but these placements have substantial minimums. The smart investor could invest through a private equity firm—again, this requires substantial minimums to gain access and the investor will have to be an "accredited investor." An "accredited investor" is a presumed sophisticated investor with a special status under financial regulation and law. An accredited investor must have a net worth of at least $1 million, not including the value of the investor's primary residence. Alternatively an investor can be accredited with an income of at least $200,000 each year for the last two years ($300,000 of combined income if married), and expect to make the same amount in the current year.

Even if the smart investor qualifies as an accredited investor, he will still need a substantial net worth and substantial investible assets to be adequately diversified if he invests in private equity offerings or makes direct private investments—minimum investment requirements could be well over $250,000. For this reason most investors could be better served using a BDC to obtain exposure to private middle market companies.

The smart investor can invest in BDCs directly by buying the shares on a stock exchange, through mutual funds, or through buying shares directly from the BDC—nontraded BDCs. Similar to nontraded REITs, our recommendation for considering nontraded BDCs stems from the low-correlated diversification advantage they offer because shares are priced through a different mechanism. Nontraded BDCs can be a little more volatile than nontraded REITs, especially debt BDCs. Debt BDCs make loans to private companies, and buy private company loans in the over-the-counter market. Many of these loans can be priced frequently, and many nontraded debt BDCs do so weekly to determine their share price. Obtaining a price for the loan portfolio is done by obtaining bids for the BDC's loans from interested buyers (banks and other institutions) as well as other valuation methods. Many of these loans are still priced in a liquid-traded market, but it is a market where only institutional investors bid. Nontraded BDCs still offer the lower correlation advantage compared to their traded cousins' shares trading on national stock exchanges. Currently there are no pure equity-focused nontraded BDCs; nontraded BDCs tend to be debt-focused, or primarily debt-focused, with small equity positions (e.g., equity "kickers").

Like nontraded REITs, nontraded BDCs could see less downward volatility in times of fear when stocks sell off. However, private company debt is priced in an institutional liquid-traded market, so it can be more volatile than physical real estate. Many nontraded BDCs have a large number of originated loans; in other words, loans the BDC negotiated directly with private companies. Although a different valuation methodology is used to value these loans their prices are affected by the bids of similar traded over-the-counter loans.

Nontraded BDCs have the same advantage as nontraded REITs in that during their open phase they have capital available that allow them to negotiate loans. Traded BDCs lack this advantage: they will have to sell loans or borrow to obtain a new loan on their books.

One difference of note between nontraded REITs and nontraded BDCs is that many prominent private equity firms have entered the field as a way to gain access to individual investors' investment capital, by offering a vehicle that doesn't have the high minimum investment amounts private equity firms require. Smart investors can now gain access to the likes of GSO/Blackstone or KKR through the nontraded BDC structure. These private equity firms are major institutional players investing billions of dollars for pension funds. Gaining access to these players' expertise through a highly regulated BDC is a major opportunity for the smart investor.

A nontraded BDC's life cycle is similar to nontraded REITs, with an open period lasting a couple of years when investor capital is raised, then a closed period when the portfolio is managed, then a liquidity event, explained below. Again, regulatory changes are taking place with regard to the pricing of nontraded BDCs which we will discuss in the future on our website www.7secretsretirement.com.

Criticism of Nontraded REITs and BDCs

We want to end this chapter by addressing the two main criticisms of nontraded REITs and nontraded BDCs: lack of liquidity, and fees. Whereas traded REITs and BDCs have daily liquidity because their shares are traded on stock exchanges, nontraded REITs and BDCs have redemption programs, when investors can sell their shares back to the issuing entity (typically once a quarter). Critics will point out these programs have two limitations. The first is that the nontraded entities could halt redemptions for any reason by a vote of their boards of directors. Nontraded REITs and BDCs might not want to offer redemptions when they will be forced to sell portfolio assets (real estate, equity positions or loans) at depressed prices. Investors could be tied up in these vehicles for years during bad market circumstances (when they are most likely to need liquidity if they haven't used our envelopes approach). The other limitation is some nontraded entities only redeem at a discount to the net asset value, often in the range of 5%.

Illiquidity

For the smart investor the issue of illiquidity of nontraded entities is crucial. Following the envelopes approach mitigates it significantly. The smart investor will have well over 15 years' worth of liquid assets in her envelopes. The lifespan of nontraded BDCs and REITs are seldom more than 10 years and often closer to seven years. Each type of investment has a similar life cycle. They have their open phase, lasting a few years, raising investor capital through the broker-dealer community, after which they close. No more investor capital is raised; they manage their portfolios of real estate or loans. To fulfill commitments in their prospectuses (and regulations), they have to provide investors a liquidity event. There are three types of liquidity events:

- ▶ A nontraded REIT or BDC could become traded by listing its shares on a stock exchange, allowing investors to sell their shares.
- ▶ Alternatively, a nontraded entity could be purchased by another entity or an institution, buying the shares of the current shareholders for cash.
- ▶ The third type of liquidity event is where the nontraded REIT or BDC could opt to self-liquidate by selling assets and distributing the cash proceeds to the shareholders. The latter process takes more time for a nontraded REIT because selling large commercial real estate properties takes months or years.
- ▶ Nontraded debt BDCs have the added option to self-liquidate by simply allowing the loans to mature, distributing the proceeds to shareholders.

For the smart investor's liquidity needs there is ample time before the capital invested in a nontraded pass-through entity will be needed if the investor follows the envelopes approach. As discussed earlier in this chapter, during periods of distress in the liquid markets investors will experience *de facto* illiquidity because they won't want to sell stocks at depressed prices. There is no practical difference between illiquidity based on choice and the illiquidity of the nontraded entities that refuse to allow redemptions due to depressed prices of their portfolio assets. We would argue that these nontraded entities inspire a useful discipline that counteracts investor fear that otherwise leads to buying high and selling low at the most inopportune times.

The one legitimate point of concern with regard to the illiquidity of nontraded entities is that if the smart investor and her advisor become disillusioned with the investment strategy of a nontraded entity, the smart investor could be stuck until the redemption window opens or a liquidity event occurs. Careful vetting should be made *before* investing in a nontraded REIT and BDC. Once the smart investor determines the percentage allocation to nontraded entities—which we recommend should be around 10% of the investor's entire portfolio, all in Envelope 3—the use of multiple entities from reputable sponsor companies could dilute the problems of being stuck in a bad investment. We still think the advantages of low-correlated diversification, and potential superior total return based on market cycles, outweigh the illiquidity concern. These are possible through REITs with substantial cash purchasing real estate, and BDCs with highly regarded private equity firms making loans.

Fees

The second major criticism is fees. We see no difference in purchasing shares of a traded BDC or REIT at a premium to their net asset value and paying a front-end capital-raising fee charged by a nontraded BDC or REIT. Also, the front load could be offset by the fact that you're investing in an entity that is making loans or buying real estate with substantial cash, which can exploit depressed asset prices and thus offer you a better return. It's hard to quantify these subjective issues. How do we know if a nontraded REIT purchasing a $300 million office building got a better deal than a traded REIT that uses more leverage? Or if a nontraded BDC negotiating the terms of a loan is getting a better deal than a traded BDC buying the loan in the over-the-counter market? We don't. That's why the issue of nontraded versus traded is not a clear-cut issue comparing apples to apples. We do know that large pension plans tend to buy physical real estate for their plans directly more often than they use traded

REITs, and that large pension plans like to buy direct private loans as opposed to using traded BDCs. Why is that? We would speculate it is because they understand the value of purchasing assets not all linked to the liquid-traded pricing mechanism of the stock market. Pension plans, with infinite time horizons, have the strongest motivation to lower their portfolios' correlations.

Conclusion

We'll summarize with the following extract from value investing investor Benjamin Graham's classic *The Intelligent Investor* where he uses the allegory of "Mr. Market" to highlight the difference in attitudes that private owners have versus owners of publicly traded shares:

> Imagine that you and Mr. Market are partners in a private business. Each day, without fail, Mr. Market quotes a price at which he is willing to either buy your interest or sell his…Mr. Market is emotionally unstable. Some days he is cheerful and can see only brighter days ahead. At other times, Mr. Market is discouraged and, seeing nothing but trouble ahead, quotes a very low price for shares in your business.
>
> Mr. Market…does not mind being snubbed. If his quotes are ignored, he will be back again tomorrow with a new quote. The investor who permits himself to be stampeded or unduly worried by unjustified market declines is perversely transforming his basic advantage into a basic disadvantage. That man would be better off if his stocks had no market quotation at all, for he would then be spared the mental anguish caused by other persons' mistakes of judgement.
>
> —as paraphrased in Robert G. Hagstrom,
> *The Warren Buffett Portfolio*, Wiley, 1999

Any nontraded investment makes ignoring Mr. Market easier.

CHAPTER 17

Other Hybrid Equity/Debt Investments

. . . .

Preferred Stock, Warrants, and Convertible Preferreds (Envelope 2 and Envelope 3)

Between debt and equity, firms have intermediate methods of raising capital. Preferred stock is the best known type of intermediate.

"Preferred" is so-called because in the hierarchy of claimants on a company's assets it falls below creditors (holders of debt instruments)—it is an equity instrument—but is preferred over common shareholders. In liquidation, after debtholders are paid, preferred shareholders have priority over common stockholders.

Preferred shares' cash flow to owners mainly comes from interest payments. Generally, they are more generous than interest on the company's bonds, to compensate for preferred's inferior creditor position. Also unlike bonds, preferred shares generally have no maturity date—interest payments continue perpetually. (However, they may be ended if the company converts preferred shares to common shares, as outlined below.) Preferreds trade on exchanges just as common shares do, usually with a ticker symbol that is a variant of the common share's symbol.

Do not let the interest feature mislead you: preferreds are still equity, and generally have a high correlation with common stocks. Their place in your portfolio is similar to that of dividend stocks, described in Chapter 14: somewhat less volatile than common stocks, but more like than unlike them as a portfolio element.

Convertible preferred shares are even more like equity. The company can convert preferred shares into common stock, at its option, when the price exceeds a designated conversion threshold. Because the buyer (you) is selling an implicit option (to convert) when you buy the shares, convertibles typically offer a slightly better interest payment than do non-convertible preferreds. But the prospect of them converting to common shares increases their correlation with common stock.

Warrants are very similar to convertible preferreds: holders receive interest payments (and no ownership) like debt, but they have the option of converting to common stock at a designated price. This is often very expensive capital from the perspective of companies issuing warrants. For example, warrants figured prominently in the federal government's 2008-09 rescue of General Motors, Chrysler, and several banks. The companies' survival was at stake, so they were obliged to accept onerous terms from their government savior.

In general, we are not advocates of these intermediate debt/equity products. They lack the investor protections of debt, and have most of the volatility of equity. The absence of maturity dates makes it very difficult to employ traditional strategies like ladders to protect against interest rate risks. Consider them in a similar category as somewhat less volatile stocks, like dividend stocks, and restrict them to a very small part of your Envelope 2, and a slightly larger part of Envelope 3.

CHAPTER 18

Other Alternative Investments
. . . .
Hedge Funds and Private Equity
(Envelope 3)

As you successfully accumulate assets, you will almost certainly fantasize about the "secret deals" that only the privileged see, such as investments in privately held growth companies, or in other asset classes that mere civilians never encounter. The most prominent of these mystique-enshrouded classes are hedge funds and private equity.

We cover hedge funds at length in our companion book, *What Hedge Funds Really Do*, so we will only summarize here. Hedge funds are private pools of capital, where the fund managers have accepted a restriction that only "accredited" (highly prosperous) investors may participate in exchange for very light regulation. Their basic goal is risk reduction. The original funds formed in the late 1940s hedged against declines in stock indexes (hence the name). As an example, a hedge fund might use its stock selection expertise to own shares in an airline, while at the same time hedging against a decline in the airline industry by shorting (betting against) the airline index.

Hedging has costs, but managers argue those costs reduce volatility, which is a primary goal of many clients.

Hedge funds are prohibited from advertising (although recent legislation may relax this restriction), so hedge fund managers shun publicity. Not coincidentally, many cultivate a mystique, implying that they use secret techniques to generate enviable returns. A few have done so: for example, Quantum Fund, one of the best known funds, has earned an average of close to 20% per year for decades and made founder George Soros a billionaire several times over.

Not surprisingly, such skills command high fees. Hedge funds, and private equity firms (described below), typically charge "2 and 20": 2% of assets as a recurring charge, similar to a mutual fund's expense ratio; and 20% of all positive returns. So if a fund returned 6% per year, managers' fees would be 3.2% = 2% plus (6% x .2). Fund managers would enjoy more than half the fund's total return. (This will be somewhat less generous for funds that specify performance payments only above a threshold like 4%.)

Undoubtedly some funds earn their fees. But as a group, hedge funds do not live up to their promise. The HFRI hedge fund index has long lagged general stock indexes. Advocates may argue that this is to be expected in a strong stock market, but there is little evidence that hedge funds as a group have offered much downside protection: the HFRI index fell nearly as far as the S&P 500 in the 2008 market meltdown.

Hedge funds' assets under management (AUM) grew significantly in the 1990s and 2000s, broadening beyond their original base of wealthy families to include as clients many institutional investment firms and pension funds. But AUM has plateaued in the $2 trillion to $3 trillion range. Increasingly, major institutions are trimming their hedge fund exposure, with CalPERS (the $300 billion California public employees' retirement system) recently joining the retreat.

Not only are fees quite high—several times those of a typical actively managed stock mutual fund, and more than 10 times those of an index fund—but hedge fund-like strategies are increasingly becoming available to retail investors through mutual funds. Such "liquid alternatives" have the advantages of hedge funds, but with the transparency and liquidity of mutual funds.

Both hedge funds and private equity are illiquid. Clients are typically heavily constrained as to when and how they can cash out. Typically they cannot sell their shares at all for at least five years, and must provide months of warning in advance when eligible to sell, to allow the fund time to unwind positions at a measured pace. These investments are candidates only for the outer edges of Envelope 3.

Private equity (sometimes known as PE) also charges 2 and 20, but invests in private companies. The goal is to improve the operations of an underperforming company in order to sell it to an acquirer, or list it publicly at a higher price that reflects its improved business results. Typically the acquisition is made with a high degree of leverage—in fact, in the 1980s these firms were known as "leveraged buyout" (LBO) firms. Major institutional investors have reduced their PE exposure also, but not to the degree of their hedge fund withdrawals.

We have made the case in Chapter 15 for investors to broaden their portfolios to gain access to middle market private companies via BDCs. The diversification and correlation advantages offered by private companies could be a reason for a high net-worth investor to seek exposure through a PE firm. We are skeptical that specifically hedge funds, and many PE investments, are truly cost-effective. They charge a great deal for the promise of superior performance (high returns, lower risk, or both). They are illiquid, and due to limited regulation, hardly shareholder-friendly. Our advice: resist the natural temptation to enter this elite club, or limit it to a very small allocation in Envelope 3. The smart investor could gain access to these asset classes through liquid alternatives bought more cheaply through mutual funds and BDCs.

Economics Nobel prizewinner Paul Samuelson, among the first to identify that the vast majority of active mutual fund managers lag their benchmark indexes, was also the first to act on that knowledge. Seeing the high profits relative to performance that mutual fund firms were earning, he invested—in the fund companies, not in their actively managed funds. If you are tempted by the sex appeal of hedge funds and private equity, buy shares in the management firms, not in the funds they offer. Several of them are publicly traded. In fact, several of their IPOs in 2007 developed to be excellent leading indicators of the stock market top.

CHAPTER 19

Inflation Hedges

· · · · · · · · · ·

Precious Metals and Commodities
(Envelope 3)

Our "new normal" posits that exploding government expenditures, including servicing debts accumulated over the past several decades, will outstrip tax revenues. Central banks will be forced to monetize government debt by printing money. When the supply of money grows faster than the economy's growth requires, excess money creation will feed into a declining value for the currency. This reduced purchasing power manifests as higher prices: inflation. Inflation is a scourge of retirees because their incomes cannot rise with prices as can wage income, and because the elderly use more of the fastest-inflating services, such as health care. So it is prudent to include in Envelope 3 assets that can be expected to rise in value faster than prices do.

Commodities of all types—agricultural products, timberland, energy, base and precious metals—are generally viewed as inflation hedges. The logic is that production of these goods is relatively fixed, so as the number of dollars expands, the prices of these scarce goods will be bid upward. But there are two problems with this overly simplified approach:

▶ High demand for commodities may be independent of inflation. When it is the result of a strong economy, accelerated inflation is possible, but not certain. Since the late 2000s inflation has remained quite tepid through an economic recovery because the velocity of money—the number of times a dollar circulates each year—crashed in 2008 and has yet to recover. The correlation between commodity demand and the CPI is far from perfect.

▶ Buying commodities is speculation, not investment. Commodities do not offer intrinsic cash flow or earnings. Any gains are strictly the result of changes in the commodity's price.

A way to counter both of these concerns is to buy stock in commodity *producers* which make commodities with natural demand—that extends outside of speculation. For example, gold is a classic precious metals inflation hedge. But gold has little intrinsic utility—even demand for gold in jewelry is highly variable. In contrast, silver has a multitude of industrial uses that expand along with the economy. And miners must compete with other mines to offer competitive returns to their owners. So buying stock in silver miners can be a true investment, not a mere speculation. Furthermore, with the significant declines in prices for precious metals since 2011, more miners are offering a (modest) dividend to keep investor interest.

The great fortunes in the California gold rush were not made by miners, but by their suppliers, such as Levi Strauss. Suppliers to industries that will thrive under inflation may have better prospects than the producers themselves. Better still are suppliers to inflation-friendly industries that enjoy tailwinds even if inflation never materializes. The broad new normal trends outlined in Chapter 5 suggest one beneficiary: agriculture, water, and suppliers to those industries. Rising incomes in developing countries are bringing a dietary shift from grains like rice, which is cheap, to meats like chicken, pork, and beef, which are not. Producing a pound of meat requires six to seven times as much grain as a pound of rice, and correspondingly more water. Suppliers to the irrigation or grain industries will enjoy rising demand for their services.

In general, we believe that inflation hedges should focus on investment, not speculation; should concentrate on producers (including suppliers), not the commodities themselves; and should emphasize those commodity industries destined to expand even without inflation.

Happily, it isn't necessary to choose specific firms to invest in. Many sector-based ETFs and mutual funds exist. You can gain exposure to a sector by buying the sector ETF or mutual fund, then concentrate on specific companies if your research commends them.

CHAPTER 20

International Investments
....
(Envelope 3)

Since the 2008–09 recession, investors around the world have been flocking to the dollar as a haven from turmoil elsewhere. But over time, the dollar, and every other developed world currency, is destined for problems. Diversifying your longer-term investments into more stable currencies may be advisable. Gains earned in stronger foreign currencies will be magnified after conversion into a shrinking dollar.

A common problem among investors is "home bias"—the tendency to overweight your portfolio with assets close to home. The GDP of the U.S is about one-fourth of the world's; absent home bias, the average investor should have only about 25% of his holdings in U.S. assets. Yet the value of all investor holdings in the U.S. is almost twice as much. This is a foolish overconcentration. Diversification into other countries and currencies is overdue.

The good news here is that you likely have more foreign exposure than you realize. Many U.S.-based multinationals derive the majority of their revenues from overseas customers. And generally, companies' operations are expanding where demographic and economic growth is happening, which is <u>not</u> in the developed world. But most of these companies' business still comes from the mature, slow-growing advanced economies. Therefore, the non-U.S. portions of your Envelope 3 should be roughly proportioned based on each country's or region's economic activity (GDP), skewed more towards future prospects than present levels.

Foreign assets have the portfolio advantage of being imperfectly correlated with equivalent U.S. assets (although correlations seem to be rising), so they can dampen swings in your overall Envelope 3.

As you expand the international share of your portfolio, this is a good place to use ETFs and mutual funds, at least to begin with. This applies to both equities and bonds. Generally, you have a choice of currency-hedged funds that buy derivatives to protect against currency risk, or unhedged funds that do not. Be careful not to be provoked into overreacting by the extra volatility caused by currency swings. But be advised that the use of currency hedges is not free; the cost will depress your average returns.

CHAPTER 21

Option Strategies for Income and Hedging

· · · · · · · · · ·

Buy/Write Funds
(Envelope 2 and Envelope 3)

One little known approach involves the use of options. These simple derivatives are often misunderstood. They suffer from guilt by association with far more complex derivative products that contributed to the financial crisis. First, we will briefly explain them.

Say that you are on vacation. You enjoy the area where you are staying, and you muse about how nice it would be to own a vacation house there. While out walking one day you stumble on a house for sale that looks very attractive. You realize that at its asking price the house will be bought quickly by some other purchaser, denying you your dream home. But you aren't prepared to make an offer yet. To tie up the house for a few weeks while you prepare your offer, you can buy an *option* from the seller. In this case, it would be a *call* option: buying the option gives you the right, but not the obligation, to "call" for the underlying asset (the house) any time before the option expires.

Movie buffs may have heard of producers "optioning" the film rights to a novel. In this situation the producer wishes to capture a book whose film potential he recognizes, but he is not yet ready to buy the film rights outright. Maybe he needs to raise production funds from investors. In this case, he could buy from the rights holder a call option on the film rights to the novel. For a defined period until the option expires, no other producer may make a film of that novel.

Owning an option confers the right, but not the obligation, to complete a transaction. Options have two components:

- ▶ A *strike price*: The price at which the option seller agrees to sell you the house if you later exercise your option;
- ▶ An *expiration date*: The date after which the option expires and the seller is no longer obligated to you.

In the vacation home example, say the asking price for the house is $250,000. You agree to pay $5,000 for the option (the option *premium*) to purchase the house for a strike price of $260,000 any time before December 31 (the expiration date). This may be an attractive proposition for both you and the option seller:

1. If real estate values stay the same or fall, you will not exercise your "out of the money" option—it will expire, worthless. The seller pockets the $5,000 you paid and can offer the house to any other buyer after your option expires.

2. If real estate prices rise and the house is worth more (say $300,000), you will probably exercise your option and buy the house for a generous discount, paying a total of $265,000 for a $300,000 property. The seller limited his upside, but made extra income through the option premium.

Options originated as a hedging device. Farmers wished to ensure predictable income from their crop despite having no control over crop prices. Speculators were willing to offer options: the speculator took the risk in exchange for income from the options premium. But any hedging strategy can be perverted into pure speculation. Options have developed a risky reputation. But they can be used to generate income with very little risk.

The general idea is to be a seller, not a buyer, of call options. Say that you own 100 shares of Intel which is currently trading at $35 per share. You can sell a call option that expires in one month at a strike price of $40, at a premium of $3 per share. One of three scenarios will occur:

1. Intel's price falls (say from $35 to $30). The call option you sold expires worthless. (No option buyer will exercise an option to buy Intel for $40 when they can buy it in the market for $30.) The option you sold softened your loss from $5 to $2.

2. Intel's price stays flat. The call option you sold expires worthless. You earned $3 in income. On a $35 stock that is almost 10%, in one month.

3. Intel soars, say to $50 per share. The call option buyer exercises his option and buys a stock worth $50 from you for $40. Selling the option capped your gain, but earned you a 10% immediate return.

Call options can be sold "covered" when you already own the underlying stock so you can supply it if it is "called away" when the option owner exercises, or "naked" when you will have to buy the shares at market price (or offer equivalent cash) to fulfill the options contract. This chapter will be restricted to selling *covered calls*, the least risky options trade and the one most suitable to novices.

Selling covered calls allow you to generate income from stocks you already hold. In effect, they magnify those stocks' dividends. They can also generate income on stocks that do not pay dividends. They are pure speculation, not investment—you already made the investment by buying the underlying stocks on which you are selling options.

You are willing to accept the options premium and in exchange make a bet that the stock's price during the period before the option expiration date will be less than the strike price. The option buyer is willing to hand over the premium in order to buy the stock at a discount if the market price exceeds the strike price before the option expires. You gain the premium, which provides income or cushions a loss. You give up gains above the strike price if the stock's price rises sharply. But since your investment focus will increasingly emphasize income over growth as you approach and enter retirement, this is not a major sacrifice.

Another low-risk options strategy of interest to value investors is selling *naked put* options. (Put options confer the right, but not the obligation, to sell the underlying security.) If you believe the intrinsic value of a stock is lower than its current price, you can sell a put option at that strike price. If the price stays high, your option will expire worthless and you pocket the premium. If the price falls, the option will be exercised and you will be obliged to buy the stock at the strike price. But that price is close to, or even below, what you believe is its intrinsic value. So you were paid by the put option buyer to wait until the stock's price fell below what you believe is a fair price; and you accepted the obligation to buy it at that price.

Naked puts are an attractive strategy for value investors who can estimate intrinsic value and are in their accumulation stage. But we will not explore this strategy further because it is of less relevance to decumulators.

For any given stock there may be a dozen options on offer at a given moment: different combinations of strike price and expiration date, each at a different premium. In general, the farther "in the money" (profitable) an option is, the higher its premium will be. Likewise, the longer the period until expiration, the higher the premium. And any transaction will need to be repeated several times a year, since most option expiration dates are no more than a few months in the future. That may seem like a lot of work for a few extra percentage points of return.

Options selling can both manage risk and augment income, but they are hardly foolproof. Options premia tend to rise and fall with market volatility. A good indicator of stock volatility is the VIX, an index of market standard deviation. Options experts often do not consider it worth the effort when the VIX falls below their specified threshold. And because options generally expire within a few months, these are not "forever" investments—at best the sales need to be repeated several times a year, involving effort and brokerage fees.

Not surprisingly, there is a way to practice option selling through a proxy. There are stock mutual funds that emphasize call writing. ("Writing" options is selling them.) While many stock funds occasionally engage in option activity, buy/write funds specialize in it. These funds have higher than average expense ratios because it is labor-intensive to research and exploit option opportunities. But they offer generous yields (income) through the options premiums they earn.

PART IV

SLEEPING WELL

CHAPTER 22

Being Stress-Free
· · · · · · · · · · ·
Jorge and Lita Rios' Financial Life Trajectory

The purpose of all the smart investing you have done, and will need to do, is *not* to build a bigger portfolio. It is to be stress-free. You want to be confident that you can continue to have the income you need once you no longer receive a paycheck. That income must be sustained under emergencies that you cannot anticipate, for a lifespan you can only guess approximately.

If all this talk of portfolios and asset classes leaves you cold, think in terms of spending, lifestyle, and avoiding 3 a.m. terrors. In this chapter we will bring together the lessons of this book in a summary of the financial life of a couple: Jorge and Lita Rios. Jorge worked as restaurant manager; Lita was a reporter and writer.

All dollar figures mentioned are in 2016 dollars, adjusted for inflation. Rough estimates of retirement income are based on a 3% withdrawal rate. This is less cautious than we recommend, but more conservative than the traditional 4% withdrawal guideline. It also ignores the possibility of a higher withdrawal rate late in retirement.

Age 25

The Rioses married at age 25, soon after they finished college. Lita became a junior reporter for a local alternative paper, making very little but building experience. Jorge managed a fast food franchise. Their combined income was $65,000. They saved about 15% of their gross income ($10,000 a year), earmarking it for a house down payment; their target was to save $50,000 by age 30. These funds are invested in a short-term bond fund.

Net worth: $20,000 Retirement income: Nil

Age 35

The Rioses live in a $250,000 house purchased with a $50,000 down payment and $200,000 mortgage. Lita joined the local daily as City Hall reporter. Jorge now manages a district of the fast food chain, overseeing a dozen stores. Their income grew smartly in their 20s and early 30s and is now $120,000 per year. They save proportionately less than in their 20s because of the expense of two kids, but they still manage to save 10% per year. Their near-term portfolio goals stress an emergency fund and beginning to save for retirement, taking advantage of retirement plans offered by their employers.

Net Worth	$70,000 in House Equity	
	$7,000 in Envelope 0 (Emergency Fund): One Month of Expenses	
	$11,000 in Envelope 3 (401(k) plans)	Potential Retirement Income: $330 per year
	$88,000 0.8 x Household Income	

Age 45

The Rioses have progressed in their careers. Lita is now city editor, and Jorge oversees a region with 50 restaurants. They are planning to offer some support to their kids' college tuition, paying about one-quarter of the cost when the kids leave for school in a few years. (They want their kids to pay something so that they take the opportunity seriously.) This expense, plus continued retirement savings, is absorbing most of their $25,000 per year in savings—about 12.5% of their combined $200,000 in annual income.

Net Worth	$150,000 House Equity	
	$60,000 Envelope 0 (Emergency Fund): Five Months of Expenses	
	$40,000 College Fund	
	$150,000 Envelope 3, Retirement	Potential Retirement Income: $4,500 per year
	$400,000 2 x Household Income	

Age 55

The Rioses are dealt some disappointments in their late 40s and early 50s. Each are laid off, fortunately not simultaneously. Lita has a cancer that costs tens of thousands and to treat it sidelined her for more than a year. Their son moved back home after graduating from college; it was almost two years before he was truly independent financially. The couple's incomes have also stagnated, with no significant raises or promotions in some years. Fortunately, their emergency fund, plus tapping (and quickly repaying) a modest amount of home equity, allowed them to weather these storms without depleting their long-term assets. Lita is concerned about her continued employability in journalism, which is consolidating. Jorge moved from a large fast food chain to a growing fast casual restaurant chain, but he also believes its market is saturating. They need to prepare for further layoffs.

Net Worth	$80,000 Home Equity (net of loan)	
	$60,000 Envelope 0 (Emergency Fund): Rebuilding—Three Months of Expenses	
	$5,000 Envelope 2	
	$300,000 Envelope 3, Retirement	Potential Retirement Income: $9,000 per year

Age 65

Happily, the Rioses have remained employed and have been able to save aggressively—25% of their $180,000 gross income—to compensate for earlier downdrafts. They paid off their home equity loan and expanded their emergency fund. They did not pay off their mortgage because its interest rate is well below the annual returns in their portfolio. They took advantage of IRS "catch-up" provisions for workers in their 50s to increase their tax-advantaged contributions in their employers' retirement plans. They have begun thinking about downsizing their home so that they can use some of their home equity.

Net Worth	$150,000 Home Equity (Loan paid off)	
	$100,000 Envelope 0 and 1 – Six Months of Expenses	
	$150,000 Envelope 2	
	$750,000 Envelope 3, Retirement	Potential Retirement Income: $30,000 per year
	$1,000,000 5.5 x Household Income	

Retirement

The Rioses are in adequate, but not ideal, shape for retirement. With a modest pension from one of Jorge's jobs, Social Security, and income from their portfolio, they can expect about $90,000 per year if they retired today—about half of their last working income. They had hoped to replace 70% to 80%. They resolve to work for up to five more years and attempt to save 40% to 50% of their income, to raise their retirement income to about $110,000. They realize that this will be the least productive saving they will ever do, because it will have the least time to compound. They resolve to invest it all in Envelope 3, where it will continue to compound until they draw down Envelopes 1 and 2 and need to replenish them—that can allow for 10 to 15 years of compounding. With the help of a financial advisor, they project their age 70 targets as:

	$ Nil	House Equity—Now omitted because it does not produce income
	$400,000	Envelope 1—Five to Seven Years' Expenses
	$400,000	Envelope 2—Five More Years of Expenses
Net Worth	$800,000	Envelope 3—Growth and Inflation Hedge
	$1,600,000	15 x Projected Household Income Projected Retirement Income: $ 48,000 per year
		Including Pension and SS: $110,000—70% of Working Income

Jorge and Lita are millionaires, but hardly feel that way. They realize that a spendable $1 million only offers about $30,000 per year in income every year for a long retirement. Even less is available as income if their assets are tied up in their home.

Conclusion

Financial advisors are known for painting rosy scenarios, of sail-boats and Caribbean vacations, to attract clients. Our hypothetical couple planned carefully, were disciplined savers and abstemious spenders—but still fell short of their aspirations because even high savings targets fell short, aggravated by a few bad breaks in middle age. Their retirement will be a compromise: they will work longer than they had hoped, and they will spend less once they no longer work. But they will be able to sleep.

Ultimately, all of your planning, past and future, isn't to amass an abstract portfolio total. It is to harvest income in that portfolio sufficient to cover your expenses. The portfolio is a means to an end, but it is the main thing you can measure to assess your progress on your way to retirement.

CHAPTER 23

Do You Need a Financial Advisor?

·········

The Truth about Financial Advice

The primary reason millions of Americans are so unprepared for retirement is because our retirement system has evolved to expect unrealistic levels of financial literacy by future retirees. A few generations ago retirees could plan on a known (often very modest) pension payment as a reward for loyalty to one employer. Today they may contribute to a bundle of retirement accounts from different employers, invested based on happenstance and whim, not a thoughtful plan.

Into this vacuum has emerged the profession of financial advisor.

This book is written by an academic who has been a client of and consultant to advisors, as well as by a financial advisor who has been active in the industry for nearly two decades. The goal of this chapter is to assist the smart investor in selecting a financial advisor by discussing the evolution of individual (retail) financial advice, explaining the current state of financial advice, and myriad conflicts of interest that exist. Complicating matters is the fact there is no standard for the use of terms like *financial advisor*, *wealth advisor*, *stockbroker, broker, financial planner, investment advisor, investment consultant,* and many other terms. Anyone offering any form of financial advice or selling financial products and insurance can use any of these titles.

Evolution of Financial Advice

The origin of financial advisors can be traced back to the stockbroker. Stockbrokers sell stocks and bonds to their clients. In the past the extent of advice was the stockbroker advising his client, "I think you should own shares of ABC Company." Most stockbrokers work for big Wall Street investment banks that are registered as *broker-dealers* with the U.S. Securities and Exchange Commission. A stockbroker working for a registered broker-dealer firm has to pass a registration exam through the Financial Regulatory Authority (FINRA) to become a Registered Representative. Brokers (Registered Representatives) have to ensure the stock or security they sell to their clients is *suitable.*

There are also *Registered Investment Advisors* (RIAs) regulated by The Investment Advisers Act of 1940 who have to register with either the Securities and Exchange Commission or the states' securities divisions. RIAs are individuals and companies who, for a fee, advise pension funds, institutions, and individuals on investment matters. (An employee of an RIA giving advice is called an Investment Advisor Representative or IAR.) The act requires RIAs and their personnel to adhere to the *fiduciary standard*, where they have to act in the *best interest* of their clients. The fiduciary standard's best interest requirement is legally a higher burden than FINRA's suitability requirement.

Evolving Regulatory Standards

These two standards have bifurcated the entire financial advisory industry in the United States. On the one hand you have Registered

Investment Advisors and their representatives following the best interest requirement providing investment advice for a fee (typically a percentage of assets under management). On the other hand you have brokers working for broker-dealers (most at large Wall Street investment banks) selling investment products, stocks, bonds, and mutual funds to their clients following the suitability requirement.

Wall Street investment banks and many other broker-dealers are dually registered, acting as both the sellers of products where they receive commissions and managing investment portfolios as Registered Investment Advisors for asset-based fees. Many financial advisors operate in this dually registered world where they provide advice for clients managing portfolios for a fee, but also, as part of the advice, place their clients in investment products that pay them a commission. Most investors are entirely oblivious to this state of affairs, and the different standards at play.

A fundamental change took place in the 1970s with the rise of the "financial planner." A financial planner differed from a broker in the sense that the financial planner emphasized a methodology of planning: setting financial goals, projecting portfolio values and retirement income, determining the appropriate asset allocation for portfolios, and managing portfolios. Financial planning encompassed a more holistic approach than merely selling stocks, bonds, and mutual funds. The first *Certified Financial Planner* designation was introduced (although nothing prevented any financial advisor from claiming to be a "financial planner"). Financial planners set up shop as Registered Investment Advisors and delivered advice and management for a fee, eschewing commissions.

As the industry created more investment products the large Wall Street firms started using the process of giving advice as the "delivery system" for their products. Employees with titles like *Wealth Advisor* or *Investment Consultant* started using some basic software programs to perform rudimentary financial planning functions. A *financial plan* would be generated and part of the plan would be recommendations for investment products. Even today, most of these plans are simplistic and cookie-cutter, serving as a delivery system for products.

Many Registered Investment Advisor (RIA) firms also performed only rudimentary planning. Here "advice" was a delivery system for gathering assets. Since these firms made their money by charging a fee for assets under management (typically in the 1% range), revenue growth had to do with gaining more assets. Many RIAs focused on selecting individual stocks and bonds based on their "proprietary" approach, and had little skills in actual financial planning.

Beginning in the 1990s, Wall Street investment banks, dually registered as broker-dealers and Registered Investment Advisors, started pushing their advisor employees to increase the proportion of fee-based advice they provide. Charging a 1% fee for assets under management provided a steady stream of residual annual revenue to these banks. This business model still allowed the banks to deliver their own products (e.g., their proprietary mutual funds) within the fee-based accounts. To adhere to the fiduciary standard, advisors couldn't exclusively use their own firms' proprietary products; however, the steady fees generated from accounts set up on the fee-based model was still preferable to the commission-only approach.

Different Types of Financial Advisors

Currently, we can distinguish among the following types of financial advisors.

- ▶ *Brokers and Agents*: focus primarily on selling stocks, bonds, mutual funds, and insurance products to clients for a commission.

- ▶ *Investment Advisors*: provide financial advice and portfolio management services for a percentage fee based on the amount of assets under their management. This is the fastest growing segment of the financial advice industry.

▶ *Financial Planners*: offer holistic and comprehensive financial planning services to clients for either an hourly fee or for a percentage fee based on assets under management (or for both). These advisors typically have some designation from an institution or university like *Certified Financial Planner* (CFP) or *Chartered Financial Consultant* (ChFC). Financial planners emphasize the "planning" component of advice, designing plans for clients covering cash flow, budgeting, savings projections, retirement income projections, asset allocation recommendations, and portfolio construction. The majority of advisors in this category end up managing the portfolios on behalf of their clients, and make most of their money from the management fees charged on the assets they manage.

▶ *Hybrid Financial Advisors*: design holistic and comprehensive financial plans for clients for a fee, managing portfolios for a fee, but also providing certain financial products for a commission.

The main factor differentiating what we call *investment advisors* and *financial planners* is the comprehensiveness of the financial planning they undertake on behalf of clients.

Admittedly there is overlap among these categories. You will find many highly competent advisors with excellent knowledge and experience focusing on comprehensive planning but who do not have any professional designations and are compensated by commissions only. These advisors should not be discarded out of hand. Conversely, there are many firms touting that they are "fee only," acting in the best interest for their clients in accordance with the fiduciary rule, but are more interested in managing and picking investments and less interested in comprehensive planning. Again, these advisors should not be disqualified for consideration by the smart investor. Investors have different levels of competencies, and different financial advice needs. There is not a one-type-fits-all approach. When it comes to planning for a stress-free retirement we feel comprehensive planning is imperative, and we are fairly agnostic as to the compensation model used by advisors.

Compensation Models and Conflicts of Interest

The smart investor should understand that financial advice is riddled by conflicts of interest. Different compensation models produce different incentives, and therefore different potential conflicts of interest between the advisor and the client. The overwhelming majority of financial advisors, irrespective of the category they fall under, are honest, trustworthy, and try and act in the best interest of their clients, regardless whether they fall under the fiduciary standard or the suitability standards. There is no compensation model that can eliminate all conflicts of interest.

Many fee-only advisors like to tout they have no conflicts of interest because they don't receive a commission—implying that the commission model is inherently conflict-ridden. The commission model has more potential conflicts of interest, but the fee-only model is hardly free of conflicts.

Advisors who only charge by the hour will always have an incentive to increase the hours spent on designing a financial plan. Their compensation model incentivizes them to always create in-depth, comprehensive, and holistic financial and investment plans for their clients. This could lead to overplanning and too many consultation meetings.

Advisors only charging a fee for assets under management has an incentive to focus their time in gathering new assets. Let's say a Registered Investment Advisor managing $100 million for clients charges an average fee of 0.75%. That equates to gross revenue to the advisor's firm of $750,000 per year. If the advisor spends all his time managing the assets and is able to increase the $100 million to $110 million, the advisor's fee will increase from $750,000 to $825,000 (a $75,000 per year increase). If we consider the average returns offered by the capital markets in the new normal, a 10% increase is no easy feat. Moreover, an advisor might do everything right and due to market dislocations the value of his assets under management might actually drop! The surest way for a fee-based advisor to stabilize revenue is to *gather more assets*. If the advisor focuses on bringing more clients on board he will get a $75,000 raise for every $10 million in new client assets being captured (assuming the market values of the assets stay the same). Asset-based fee advisors are incentivized to gather more assets, not to prepare comprehensive plans.

These advisors are also incentivized not to spend too much time on activities unrelated to managing their portfolios. For instance, there is no incentive to spend time convincing clients to move money into an insurance policy for estate planning purposes. The advisor can't receive a commission for insurance products, so the move will lower assets under their management, effectively bringing a pay cut. This presents a conflict because for many investors, using insurance products to fund trusts as part of estate planning is in their best interest.

Asset-based fee advisors also do not have an incentive to use products like credit union or online bank CDs. Again, they will lose assets and get a pay cut.

Financial planners designing comprehensive plans and working under the asset-based fee model face similar incentives. Although some charge a fee upfront for their plans, they still receive disproportionate compensation from asset-based fees, incentivizing them to gather assets and ignore products not designed for fee-based accounts. Most annuity-type investments discussed in Chapter 12 can only be purchased through the commission model. These products may be ignored by the financial planner, or at best, no great effort is exerted to get the client to purchase an annuity from an agent or broker.

A massive incentive exists for a commission-based financial advisor to sell clients products with the highest commissions or to trade frequently (churning) to generate trading commissions.

Similar incentives exist to focus more on gathering assets than comprehensive planning ("plans" are often mere delivery systems for products). Commission-based advisors might overdo allocations to variable annuities, active mutual funds, and other esoteric high-paying commissionable products.

Do I Need a Financial Advisor?

Given the criticisms we've discussed in this chapter, you may rightfully ask, "Should I even work with an advisor?" and "How can I chose a trustworthy advisor?"

One of the authors is a financial advisor, which biases some of our discussion. We hope this bias is offset by the other author being an academic with a reputation to protect. To address the question about needing a financial advisor we contend that the changing landscape facing retiring baby boomers (discussed in Chapters 1 to 5), coupled with the complexities of designing investment portfolios for retirement (Chapters 6 to 9), make a strong case that almost all smart investors will need some form of personalized advice. Building a financial plan based on the envelopes approach that will provide sustainable income for the rest of your life is complex. Selecting among the different investment vehicles (products) from the list discussed in Part III adds another layer of complexity. Maintaining the envelopes—deciding when to refill certain envelopes and with which assets—adds a final level of difficulty. It is hard to see how even the smartest investor can negotiate this complex maze without some help.

Choosing Your Advisor

The key in selecting an advisor is to do your homework. Reading this book is an important first step in the process. Taking responsibility to educate yourself about different products, the different categories of advisors, and the differences among how they are compensated, will arm the smart investor with information to help make a wise choice when selecting a financial advisor. We recommend interviewing multiple financial advisors and engaging at least two to design a plan for you. A novel approach we like is to have both advisors present their plans together. You should use the design and presentation of the financial plan as an "interview" process.

Don't get too caught up by the compensation model employed by an advisor. It will always be more expensive to use the services of an advisor than to do it yourself. The advisor has to be paid in some way for the value he or she adds. You should ask them hard questions about their chosen compensation model. If you're considering a commission-only advisor, let the advisor address your concern about being "sold" high-commissionable products. Talk about the issue of suitability versus best interest and how the advisor address the issue. When interviewing a fee-only advisor, ask about insurance products like variable annuities or certain life insurance policies and why they are not part of the proposal.

Simply because potential conflicts of interest exist within each category of financial advisors doesn't mean advisors in a particular category or following a specific compensation model are automatically subject to these conflicts and incentives. The overwhelming majority of advisors are respectable people who offer smart investors much needed help. Remember, the most important incentive for any advisor is *to keep his clients*. Client retention is the surest way advisors can build wealth for themselves. Clients stay with advisors when they have a high degree of trust in them.

Clients who are satisfied also stick with their advisors. Satisfaction is a product of trust, which in turn grows out of the feeling that the advisor is acting in the investor's best interest (regardless of legal definitions). Over the long run, advisors cultivating trust are the most successful, retaining their clients and their assets, receiving referrals from their clients, and having their clients serve as references for prospective new clients. In this broad sense, most financial advisors' interests are aligned with their clients' interest.

We have our preferences (and biases) when it comes to advisor selection. As mentioned, we prefer hybrid advisors (those providing services and products for both fees and commissions). There are many products and investment vehicles smart investors should use which are only available to purchase with a commission. Why exclude these products just because they can't be accommodated within a fee-based model? Dividing your portfolio amongst accounts or envelopes, some of which you will be charged based on commissions and some based on an asset-fee, could be more affordable over time. It's cheaper to pay a 2% or 3% commission to invest in a structured CD or fixed index annuity with a five-year maturity in Envelope 2 than 1% per year in an asset fee over five years.

We prefer advisors with a proven track record of designing comprehensive plans. We also prefer advisors who have a Certified Financial Planner or Chartered Financial Consultant designation. There are numerous professional designations, many of which are not hard to obtain (i.e., have very low standards). The CFP and ChFC designations are two with the highest standards to achieve. This does not mean an advisor without one of these prestigious designations should not be considered. Experience still counts.

We have a preference for a team of advisors (two or more). This is predicated on the expectation that a team will share ideas and challenge each other. Comprehensive financial planning and investment management are a broad field, so an advisory team of diverse specialists can complement each other. A true team is one in which the two or three advisor team members do not have separate clients. They serve their clients together.

Given the growing challenges from "macro" developments that we have termed the new normal, advisors with an academic background in macroeconomics, global finance, or political economy are preferable. After all, portfolios are constructed and managed within a global political and economic context.

When financial advisors take you through their planning process, presenting their different plans, you will get a sense of the quality of the advisors or advisory team. Coupled with your own homework, probing them about their compensation models and how they address the conflicts of interest inherent to those models, you will enhance your sense of trust with one of the advisors. Finally ask for references. In the end when you've narrowed it down to two, if you can't decide, pick both. It is ideal to work with only advisors or a team from one firm; however, at first it could be helpful to work with two advisors or advisory teams from two firms. At some point, you will gravitate to one of them.

If You Are a Knowledgeable Investor

Smart investors recognize the value of knowledge and have a keen interest in planning. You would not be reading this book otherwise. Your greatest reservation about advisors may be a belief that your aptitude in planning makes an advisor redundant, and his fees wasted.

This is understandable, but misguided. Just as attorneys who represent themselves have a fool for a client, you will be too close to your own situation to maintain proper perspective. Doctors do not "need" to consult colleagues to treat themselves or their family members, but most acknowledge the value of a second opinion.

Here are some of the main ways an advisor can add value to your retirement planning, from the most elementary to the more subtle:

▶ *Estimating your long-term income needs*. While Chapter 1 gives you the tools to make a rough estimate by yourself, an advisor can customize it to your special circumstances, such as other financial needs besides retirement (e.g., college tuition, or financial support for aging parents), your tolerance of risk, or the riskiness of your sources of wage income.

▶ *Compute gaps between your assets and your aspirations* to advise you on any increased savings you must undertake, well before you need the funds (so that compounding has time to operate).

▶ *Estimating your probability of success.* Many advisors have access to historical data on investment returns that allows them to run your retirement scenarios under many alternative assumptions. The averages cited in this book are just that. Your sleep will be less encumbered if you knew that your plan worked—that is, your money did not run out before your death—in worse than average situations, like a prolonged bear market. Monte Carlo simulation can project your assets and income over thousands of combinations of annual returns from recorded history, to determine the fraction of them where your plan succeeds. The higher the fraction, the sounder you can sleep. Personally, we prefer plans that can be expected to work—where you die before your portfolio is depleted—in at least 95% of analyzed scenarios.

▶ *Recommend a portfolio allocation to achieve your retirement goals at the lowest possible risk.* Numerous studies have demonstrated that almost all investing return is driven by the *allocation* among assets, rather than the *selection* of specific assets.

▶ *Screen and recommend specific investments pursuant to an over-arching plan.* The new normal and the envelopes strategy both mandate that you include assets, like alternatives (REITS, BDCs, MLPs, etc.), that diverge sharply from traditional stocks and bonds. In fact, that divergence is one of their attractions. While you may have knowledge about some asset classes like stocks or stock mutual funds, a diverse portfolio allocated among multiple asset classes will inevitably span far beyond your circle of competence. An advisor who is knowledgable where you aren't and who is backed by a substantial due diligence process can screen candidate investments that have a place in your plan.

▶ *Educate you about unfamiliar concepts and options.* Any good service provider must be an effective teacher. Any principled one welcomes clients who crave education, and considers educating clients one of the most enjoyable parts of the job. While advisors can be quite expensive tutors (and you can find similar education less expensively in books, publications, lectures, and online), there will certainly be areas where you will need customized education. Be wary of any advisor who seems unable or reluctant to teach you.

▶ *Be your asset allocation conscience.* If you pay attention to the financial world, you will inevitably hear about tempting new products, or feel impelled to play hunches about trends. You may also panic in a downturn and wish to completely exit some risky asset class. An advisor can keep you objective by reminding you of your plan and target asset allocation.

▶ *Rebalance.* Over time your portfolio's asset proportions can deviate from your targets when returns diverge. Research shows the importance of *rebalancing*—selling some of the overweighted asset to buy some of the underweighted one—periodically to return your allocations to their target levels. This is a way to "sell high and buy low" without explicitly timing markets. Most of us are terrible at this: we get distracted by other tasks, or we linger too long with the successful assets and are reluctant to increase our holdings of the lagging asset. An advisor can exercise the discipline that many of us lack.

▶ *Undertake ignored but necessary tasks.* Many of us devote our financial time to the sexy stuff like investing, but give little attention to prosaic but critical tasks like establishing an emergency fund, securing appropriate levels of insurance, and preparing a will and an estate plan. Accountability to an advisor who is attentive to these tasks increases the chance they will actually be executed.

Chances are that you saw yourself in some of the above. The advisor you need will depend on the areas that will most complement your strengths and compensate for your weaknesses.

A common failing of advisors' clients is that they pay for a plan and then ignore it. To get your money's worth, you must commit to following through on an advisor's plan.

Many financial plans become expensive coasters on the client's coffee table. When Eisenhower was Supreme Allied Commander in Europe he said, "Plans are nothing; *planning* is everything," and he was right. Do not treat this as an exercise you can completely outsource. You need to personally invest time and attention so that you live your plan going forward.

Advisors for Every Client

In Romero's case, when he undertook a search for an advisor, he did not have much need for an overarching plan, although he welcomed a "second opinion" review of the one he had created himself. But he identified three basic personal weaknesses that an advisor could complement:

▶ *Screen for low-correlation asset classes, such as alternatives and insurance products.* As he reflected on the new normal (as discussed in Chapter 4), he realized that alternative investments needed to be a much larger part of his portfolio. He sought an advisor who has special expertise in alternative investments and insurance strategies and someone with an excellent screening process to identify candidate investments.

▶ *Maintain target asset allocation*: Romero realized that he could inadvertently exceed reasonable asset allocation targets as he pursued his macro hunches. He needed an outside person to limit his enthusiasms and keep his asset allocations in bounds.

▶ *Rebalance and execute*: Discipline is not a hallmark of Romero's investing behavior! Often he considers a task accomplished when he understands it, rather than completes it. He is willing to pay an advisor to handle the mundane details like rebalancing, and to actually execute trades needed to implement and maintain his plan.

Your own self-assessment may be quite different. The exercise is very worthwhile, because it will offer good guideposts as to what skills you need most in an advisor. Otherwise, you may pay for services you do not really need.

The Missing Criterion: Outperformance

As noted earlier, only a vanishingly small number of fund managers outperform their benchmarks over the long term. The chances of an advisor who serves retail clients doing so is even less. *Cross off your list any advisor whose value proposition is based on outperformance.* Most advisors are realistic about this, but some aren't.

The most common version of this claim amounts to pretensions of clairvoyance: the advisor (or newsletter writer, or hedge fund manager) claims he has had some proprietary technique that allows him to see the future so he can anticipate trends to profit from them. The technique is quite secret, or at least shrouded in mystery. Stated this way it sounds ludicrous, and it is.

Protecting Yourself

Bernard Madoff's clients operated in blissful ignorance, until they couldn't. Madoff claimed to earn highly stable returns, producing account statements to corroborate his magic. Of course, it was all a sham: he operated a Ponzi scheme, paying old investors with new investors' funds, until the 2008 meltdown shut off the supply of new investors. Those account statements were completely fraudulent.

Regardless of your indifference to your portfolio, you owe it to yourself to use only advisors who custody your funds at an independent institution. Review that institution's statements as well as any separate ones provided by your advisor to identify discrepancies. Ask questions and arm yourself with a basic background understanding so that you can spot any moonshine an unscrupulous advisor tries to sprinkle. These steps are not foolproof. Clever crooks, like Madoff, can conceal misdeeds at grand scales for long periods of time. But no one will guard your interests better than you.

Regulatory Changes

Important regulatory changes are in the process of transforming the financial advisory industry. In April 2016, after years in the making, the Department of Labor released its much anticipated fiduciary rule. With this regulation, coming into effect April 2017, financial advisors must adhere to the fiduciary standard's best interest principle when providing advice on IRA or other retirement assets. It does away with the lower suitability standard. This rule is a game-changer in the way advice will be delivered. The rule allows advisors to continue receiving commissions for certain products under an exemption, as long as the advisor enters into a binding contract that the commissionable product is in the best interest of the client. At this stage it is unclear what impact this far-reaching rule will have. Some broker-dealers might transform themselves into Registered Investment Advisors only offering fee-based services due to the onerous compliance requirements to offer commissionable products through the best interest contract exemption. Some products might not be available in retirement accounts. We will provide updates regarding this rule and its impact on our envelopes approach at www.7secrets-retirement.com.

CHAPTER 24

Recovery

While this book has been written for smart investors, no one is immune from mistakes. Boomers have made more than their share regarding retirement planning: Millions have very little in savings and no real idea when and how they can retire. If you are one of that large majority, in this chapter we will offer a few ideas on how to recover.

We will not insult your intelligence by claiming that these ideas will fund your "dream retirement." It simply isn't possible to make up in a few months for decades of not saving. But this chapter can help you begin the road to recovery. In particular, it will provide some safety warnings about common mistakes that some desperate boomers make.

Delaying Social Security

Many have misled themselves into assuming that their retirement income needs will be met by Social Security, and by extension by other pension income such as your employer's pension. This is a dangerous supposition.

Social Security was designed to prevent poverty among the elderly, not to offer a middle-class income. Average payouts are less than 30% of average working incomes. If you have worked for an unusual number of years you may see slightly more than the average, but it will never be greater than about $35,000 per year. This is a gross figure, which will be significantly less if your benefits are highly taxed.

Pensions are a dying vehicle: Less than one in five private sector workers can expect a defined benefit pension. All pensions, including Social Security, are groaning under the weight of demographics. Their finances were designed in an era when workers contributed for 20 to 30 years, then received benefits in retirement for five to 10 years. But because of lengthened lifespans, retirements can last for 30 years or longer. Most retirement plans are significantly underfunded (i.e., they have not amassed enough assets to pay out anticipated benefits). Social Security's fiscal condition gets a great deal of media attention, especially in election years, but many other government and private pension plans are in worse shape. Finally, if the pension is offered by an organization that can legally declare bankruptcy, that declaration can allow the company to renounce their financial obligations, including cutting or eliminating pension payouts *in toto*. It is prudent to accumulate assets to replace at least part of the pension income you expect, because there is a good chance it will evaporate. (For private pensions there is some insurance up to certain low limits through the Pension Benefit Guarantee Corporation, which is a federal agency.)

The most common mistake retirees make is *beginning to collect Social Security too early*. The law establishes "full retirement age" (FRA) based on your year of birth (currently, FRA is about age 66; it extends by a few months each year). If you begin collecting at that age, you will receive the monthly benefit estimated in the annual statement you receive from the Social Security Administration. But you can begin collecting benefits *at a reduced rate* as early as age 62. The math is straightforward: the SSA projects a total lifetime benefit for each recipient. If you start earlier, your monthly payment must be reduced to keep within that projected total benefit.

The same logic applies in reverse if you delay beginning collection: Each year of delay, up until age 70, increases your benefit—specifically by about 8% per year of delay. An 8% *inflation-adjusted, risk-free* return is unheard of in today's investing environment.

Many people who lost their jobs in their early 60s during the 2008-09 recession immediately filed to begin collecting Social Security. If this happens to you and you have no alternative, we sympathize and wish you well. But do not elect this option voluntarily until you have exhausted all alternatives.

Start planning by educating yourself about how Social Security works and your options for stretching your benefits. Register for an online account with the SSA at www.socialsecurity.gov/myaccount. Choose your financial advisor in part based on his or her proficiency with Social Security or other pension options.

Work Longer

Unless you are forced into retirement, you have an active choice about when you stop working. We want to urge you to stay in the workforce a while longer, if you can.

Financially, the arithmetic is undeniable: Each year of work allows you to accumulate more assets, and decreases the length of time you will be decumulating later. Millions of boomers have been obliged to continue working (e.g., if their spouse was laid off in the recession), which is arguably unintentionally smart. But there are other, nonfinancial arguments discussed below.

First, leaving the workforce in your 50s or 60s is effectively irreversible. Regardless of legal sanctions, age discrimination is very real. Employers who are Gen Xers or millennials perceive boomers as being inflexible and unable to adapt to new technologies and business models. And even if you are able to become reemployed after "retiring," it will probably be at a significantly lower wage than before you retired. For the past generation average incomes have been flat or declining; only a tiny fraction of workers at the top of the spectrum have made economic progress. Growing competition from three billion new capitalists—part of the new normal described early in the book—has suppressed wages in many middle-income occupations. If you can land a job, the one you secure is much more likely to pay near-minimum wage than your old, pre-retirement salary. If you are still working, chances are you have mastered the job's challenges; you are highly productive and can command a fair salary. You lose that edge in a new job.

Working longer also has health and longevity benefits. Numerous gerontological studies have shown that seniors who experience the mental challenge, social interaction, and self-esteem that comes from accomplishment at work are happier, healthier, and live longer.

We understand that retirement may be forced on you by circumstance. Keeping your skills honed and contributing to your employer's success provide some protection. You can also make contingency plans to use your skills to be your own boss in an entrepreneurial venture if you are laid off from a salaried position. Being a freelance teacher, writer, or accountant can keep you active and employable and allow you to expand or contract your work effort at your discretion once work is no longer a financial necessity.

Keeping a Lid on Risk

Excessive risk-taking is distressingly common among pre-retirees, especially when investors are lulled to complacency by a bull market. It is especially dangerous if you have not saved enough. It can escalate a problem into a personal crisis.

As we argued earlier in the book, it is prudent to reduce the volatility of your portfolio by trimming risky equities and substituting more stable, slower-growing assets in the years leading to retirement. But many who did not save enough instead increase their portfolio's risk in the hope of earning a "big score." Often, familiar investments breed misplaced confidence: If you have made good returns in real estate, or in a private business, why not double down to turbocharge your portfolio's overall return?

The arguments about portfolio overconcentration mimic those about leverage: both magnify gains when your optimistic hopes are realized—and deliver crippling losses when they are not. Ask anyone with leveraged real estate holdings in 2008, when "house prices always rise"—until they didn't.

The greatest investors have concentrated their investments intensively. Bill Gates became the world's richest man through his ownership of one company, Microsoft. Warren Buffett often keeps 40% or 50% of Berkshire Hathaway's investments, like its Buffett Partnership predecessors, in only three or four stocks. But these men had exceptional ability to identify great businesses, and the financial reserves and patience to ride out steep downdrafts. They also invested at the right time, when the asset was cheap. Unless you can be confident you have similar skills, overconcentration is likely to aggravate your financial challenges, not solve them.

The problem with a truly diversified portfolio—where no single asset is more than, say, 5% of your total—is even a few home runs will add only modestly to your overall score. If you are seriously moved to bet on speculative ventures, do it only with amounts you can lose without tears—say 1% or 2% of your assets. If you need every dollar to work in order to make up for lost time (saving), even this may be too aggressive.

Downscaling, Including Overseas

If your assets won't provide enough income to meet your retirement aspirations, one option is to downsize your aspirations. Lower one or more of the major expenses you will face in retirement. The largest expenses are generally health care and housing.

To cut these costs several million Americans have already expatriated (relocated out of the U.S.) or are actively considering it. Once you are no longer tethered to a location due to employment, you are free to live anywhere. A rich network of advisors and promoters exists to help you educate yourself about overseas living opportunities. Many countries such as Panama and Costa Rica actively recruit *Norteamericanos* to retire there, with generous health care systems (often staffed with English-speaking providers), expedited visa and residency programs, and tax incentives. One national incentive program is called *pensionado*, leaving no doubt about its target market!

If you wish to remain in the U.S., you can still cut your expenses by moving to a region with a significantly lower cost of living, as thousands have done. For higher-income retirees, one of the eight states that has no income tax may be especially attractive since taxes may be one of your largest expenses. You can also cut your retirement expenses by paying off your mortgage by retirement time, either by accelerating payments while working, refinancing into a shorter-term mortgage at a lower interest rate, or downsizing to a less expensive home that you buy with only home equity in your former home.

These are all momentous life changes, and we do not wish to minimize the changes they entail. But they are much less risky than the ill-advised ones mentioned above.

CHAPTER 25

For 20-, 30- and 40-Somethings

This book has been written primarily for those smart investors whose retirement is fairly imminent. If yours is still decades away, you may be the smartest investor of all since you can use this knowledge to plan your middle years. You deserve a chapter of your own.

You have an enormous advantage over those a generation older; you have time to prepare, and time to let compounding work for you. In terms of portfolio planning, you should generally follow what earlier we called the "conventional wisdom." Save aggressively, invest in equities, diversify through mutual funds and ETFs, and gradually reduce your equity exposure as you approach retirement. This is a lifelong task. Here are a few things you can do this year to start you on your promising path as a smart investor.

Estimate Your Retirement Income Requirement

If you don't know where you are going, you won't know when you get there. Millions of your parents and grandparents did not save enough because they never did the basic arithmetic. Review Chapter 1 for a general guide. If all or nearly all of your retirement income will need to come from your own assets—very likely as the few remaining pensions fade into oblivion—plan on amassing 20 to 30 times your target income. In round numbers this will require you to have accumulated about 10x to 15x your wage income by age 45, adding about an additional 5x each decade thereafter through continuous savings and investment growth.

Really "Get" the Arithmetic of Compounding

Early in the book we introduced you to the power of compounding in the story of two twin sisters: one invested early and stopped early, while the other started late and invested continuously thereafter. The frugal sister ended up with a nest egg over 50% larger—*because it had compounded for 10 years longer*. Everyone we have met who has been exposed to this comes away profoundly changed (including us). Warren Buffett, for instance, has very frugal habits because he realized very early that spending $1,000 now forecloses about $10,000 in a decade.

Buffett and Berkshire Hathaway have earned nearly 20% per year for six decades. Your returns are almost certainly not as impressive, so compounding's effects aren't quite as dramatic. But simply holding a diversified basket of stocks like an index fund has doubled its value in seven years, increased by eightfold in 20 years, and by thirtyfold in 35 years.

Run a spreadsheet to project a portfolio at a few hypothetical rates of return. Learn the "Rule of 72." Really "get" the power of compounding. Self-discipline will not seem so difficult when you realize that your $4 daily latte that costs you $1,000 a year now is robbing you of the price of a good new car in retirement—*every year*.

Save More

These aggressive wealth milestones can be met if you start early and let the power of compounding turbocharge your assets. But the engine needs fuel—you need to save significantly, especially in your early years (when compounding has the most time to work its magic). Planners talk about savings rates in the range of 10% to 15% of gross income. We recommend even more, like 25% in your 20s and early 30s, gradually relaxing to 10% to 15% by around age 40.

All of this savings does not need to be earmarked for retirement; it can reasonably be devoted to any appreciating asset, including a primary residence or a university degree. Just be honest with yourself about which purchases are actually assets that produce a return (income), and which are really consumption.

Get Off the Hedonic Treadmill

If you observe friends and coworkers after they get a raise, you will usually see them react in the following stages:

- ▶ Glee
- ▶ Satisfaction—at being validated
- ▶ Indulgent—enjoying spending extra
- ▶ Irritated—at their higher tax bill
- ▶ Confused—at how their glee evaporated so quickly

Economists call this the "hedonic treadmill": More income leads to more spending, but more spending generates little added happiness. We quickly become accustomed to our new spending level. Better to save your raises now to buy you peace of mind later. An added bonus is that if you do not enhance your lifestyle with each raise, you will need to replace less income when you retire.

Try a Budget

Only a small fraction of Americans budget their expenses. So it isn't surprising that the majority of households spend every dollar they earn—and often more.

When you retire, you will lose the ability to make up for unexpected expenses by working harder. So it is a good idea to gain the habit of spending within a constraint. Build a simple budget. It need not be elaborate; in fact, it is easier for you to conform if it has only a few, broad expense categories. Begin cultivating the habit of discipline early, so that it will be thoroughly ingrained when you really need it. This may also help you estimate your real income needs in retirement, and give you useful insight into how to implement the envelopes strategy.

Put It on Autopilot

Psychologist Daniel Kahneman won the 2002 Nobel prize in Economics for his work (with Amos Tversky) explaining how real people make real financial decisions, as opposed to how economists theorize decisions are made. In his *Thinking, Fast and Slow* he argued that we all have two cognitive systems: System II is careful and deliberative, relying on evidence and logic (*slow*), while System I is intuitive and mercurial—and *fast*. But engaging System II involves mental effort that no one has in unlimited supply. So we often fall back on System I, that uses shortcuts and rules of thumb (that Kahneman calls heuristics)—and often is wrong. As a result, we often default to whatever the status quo is.

If you need to deliberate over each dollar whether to save or spend it, you will save less. Employers who establish a default retirement contribution for their employees find that large fractions never change it because it takes too much effort. So retirement plans are increasingly setting as their defaults a low but meaningful contribution rate, and a target date fund as the default plan. Under this default overall employee contribution rates rise, and employees' assets are more sensibly allocated. This is because saving and investing were put on automatic.

Financial advisors commonly say "pay yourself first" instead of saving only what is "left over" after spending, which is often nothing or very little. They argue you should designate the first use of your paycheck to investing, leaving only what is left over to spending. Payroll deductions, such as those taken to pay taxes, make this process automatic. No mental energy is needed to save and invest each pay period.

Your employer may set a default contribution rate, probably a low number like 3% of your gross pay. Do not assume that amount is right for you; chances are it is too low. At least, set it to the maximum amount that your employer matches, if you are fortunate and have an employer match available (many went extinct in 2008). For your investment election, take the target date fund option that comes closest to your likely retirement year, or a bit later. That assures your asset allocation will be automatically adjusted over time. The idea is to put savings and retirement investing on autopilot, until the day when you are ready to focus on it. In the meantime, use the reports you receive from your account custodian as a way to begin educating yourself about investing, so you can decide if you wish to take more control. But until you do, or if you *never* do, you'll know that your retirement savings are moving in the right general direction.

Forewarned Is Forearmed

You are taking an important step towards being a smart investor by beginning your education now. You should continue this lifelong process. Even if you engage a financial advisor, you should never rely solely on that person. Your knowledge will help protect you against charlatans and allow you to assess if the professional's advice is in your best interest.

CHAPTER 26

Conclusion

The financial industry's stock and trade is greed or fear. Many investment firms advertise their services with backdrops of plush vacation homes or Caribbean vacations. When markets turn down the ads may replace sailing excursions with scenes of cold water walkups with funereal dirges as background music. Nothing wrong with this: marketers do their best work when they capture the *zeitgeist* of their targets.

Our mission in *It's the Income, Stupid!* was neither to feed your greed nor provoke your anxiety. We simply want you to be realistic. After a multiyear bull market and following a generation-long historical success story for asset prices, it is only prudent to deemphasize offense and instead build your defenses. Less growth, more income. Even if you do not believe any of our thoughts about the future's new normal, every year you *will* get a year older, and your risk tolerance will erode.

We recognize that making an about-face with your portfolio isn't easy. The personal qualities that made you a great accumulator need to be adapted for decumulation. That is the goal of our main framework, the envelopes approach.

Envelopes in Summary

The core idea is one that is familiar to you. You already earmark some funds for specific expenses. You may have a "vacation fund" or a "pay off the mortgage fund." The envelopes approach is a generalization of this idea. Instead of treating your entire portfolio as a single agglomeration, it breaks it into several envelopes, each with successive time horizons (times in the future when you will need the money). Our illustrations assumed three envelopes in retirement, with horizons of five, 10 and 15+ years. Combining all your assets together was reasonable when you were accumulating for one giant, long- range goal (retirement). But when that day arrives, separating your funds among those you will need in the next few years—whose principal must be protected at the expense of return—versus those you will not need for at least a decade—and can be invested for growth and inflation hedging—can make your money last the longest. This has been extensively validated by investment research.

We outline a three-envelopes program:

▶ Envelope 1 holds the funds you will need to meet expenses over the next five years. Its focus is on principal protection.

▶ Envelope 3 holds the bulk of your assets, invested for growth.

▶ If you wish, an intermediate Envelope 2 can be the buffer between the other two envelopes.

On the risk/return spectrum of investment choices shown in Chapter 3, Envelope 1 should concentrate in the lower left quadrant, Envelope 3 in the upper right, and Envelope 2 (if you choose to have one) in the middle of the efficient investing frontier.

As you spend down Envelope 1 you replenish it from the other envelopes. In Chapter 6 we outline three alternative principles for refilling Envelope 1 and suggest our favorite.

Our five-year breakpoints aren't sacrosanct. We offered some principles so that you can customize this schedule to your own needs.

Putting Envelopes Into Practice

So where do you start? First, if you are still working, your absolute most urgent priority is none of these. It is creating an Envelope 0— an emergency fund—with enough funds to cover your expenses during a period of unemployment. Some advisors suggest six months' of expenses are sufficient, but we believe that at least one year, and closer to two years, is prudent. A large Envelope 0 ceases to be necessary once you stop working, since you will no longer need to replace working income. (Said better, you will be doing so continually through the other envelopes.)

After Envelope 0, you should continue to build your envelopes in numerical order. Next priority should be the principal-protected Envelope 1; then the hybrid Envelope 2; and finally the growth Envelope 3.

How much to allocate to each envelope is determined by your annual spending needs and the time horizons you choose. If you need to spend $50,000 per year then your Envelope 1 should hold about $250,000 in principal-protected investments like money market funds, CDs, single premium annuities, and short-term bonds that can become liquid on a known schedule. Envelope 2 would be of a similar size, invested in moderate risk and income-oriented assets such as fixed annuities, fixed index annuities, medium-term bonds, variable annuities with protected income bases, and dividend-oriented stock funds. The remainder of your portfolio would be in Envelope 3, invested for growth in stocks, stock mutual funds and ETFs, index funds, REITs, BDCs, and MLPs. At first this envelope might require the fewest changes, since almost all of your retirement portfolio is probably in Envelope 3-type assets.

Your overall allocation will depend on the size of Envelope 1, which in turn determines Envelopes 2 and 3. Your goal is to smooth your consumption: to keep your real (after inflation) income about constant over time. If you plan your portfolio for a 30-year retirement—conservatively assuming a long life—then your first five years of spending in Envelope 1 should hold about 16% of your assets, as should your next five years in Envelope 2. The next 20 years (two-thirds of your assumed 30-year remaining lifespans) would be in Envelope 3, 66% of your total. But amounts are far more important than percentages. Fully load Envelopes 1 and 2, and if necessary stint on Envelope 3, knowing that it has considerably more time to grow. But put a sizable fraction of your portfolio—we suggest at least 50%—in Envelope 3, unless you expect to live for less than 10 more years.

Assets for Envelopes

Table 26.1 on the next page summarizes the various types of investments discussed in previous chapters and their role in each envelope. Note that these assignments are for a "typical" retiree. You may be anything but typical. That is where good advice can offer reassurance.

Each row is a type of investment, identifying the chapter(s) where it was discussed. Each column is an envelope. In the cells of the table are one of three symbols. A blank means the asset isn't suited for that envelope. "++" means it is a central option for that envelope—it should play a major role. "+" means it is a secondary option for that envelope, and should pay a lesser role.

This table is highly simplified, since there are many varieties of each investment type, with somewhat different goals and characteristics. Simply because a given class is recommended does not mean that every specific asset in that class is right for that bucket. As mentioned in Chapter 24, this is where your advisor can earn her fees: by screening among a group of, say, REITs to identify those well suited to your specific plan and situation. Chapters 10 through 22 provide primers on each asset class and its role in the envelopes strategy.

As you can see, the lower return/risk assets generally are more suited to Envelopes 0 or 1, and the opposite ones are better for Envelope 3. Intermediate risk/return assets can be very appropriate for Envelope 2. Envelope 3 consists of growth investments, but should have healthy doses that are designed to generate income like REITs

Table 26.1 Investment Types in Each Envelope

Investment Type	Chapter(s)	Envelopes				Remarks
		0	1	2	3	
Money market funds	7, 10	++	++			Low risk/low return
CDs, Short-term bonds	7, 10		++	+		Low risk/low return
Structured CDs	7,10		++	++		Principal protected
Mid- and Long-term bonds	9, 10			++	+	Moderate risk
SPIAs	7, 12		++	+		Longevity protection
Fixed annuities	7, 12		++	+		Insurance company "CD"
Fixed index annuities	7, 12		+	++		Similar to structured CD
Dividend stocks	9, 14			+	++	It's all about the income
Variable Annuities	9, 12			++	+	Protected Income Base
Return of Principal "Annuity"	9, 12			++	+	Not really an annuity
REITs: traded	8, 15, 16				++	Alternative investment
REITs: non-traded	8, 15, 16				++	Illiquid Alternative
BDCs: traded	8, 15, 16				++	Alternative Investment
BDCs: non-traded	8, 15, 16				++	Illiquid Alternative
Stocks and stock mutual funds	8, 11				++	Growth/inflation hedge
Tactical funds	11			+	++	Go anywhere funds
Private equity	18				+	Small allocation
Hedge funds	18				+	Consider liquid alts
Glide path/Target date funds	21					For accumulation phase
International stocks & funds	11				++	Prevent home-bias
Index stock funds	11				++	Growth/inflation hedge
Viaticals	13			+	+	Small allocation
Commodities	19				+	Greater risk/return
Hybrid equity/debt	17			+	+	Preferreds/warrants
Options	21				+	Buy/write funds
ENVELOPE GOALS	0 — Emergency fund; liquid, principal-protected					
	1 — Short-term spending; principal-protected; predictable					
	2 — Buffer; income-producing					
	3 — Growth and inflation-hedging					

or BDCs, or funds that hold them, as well as dividend stocks and funds. Remember, it's the *income,* stupid!

Envelopes and Taxes

Your phasing of withdrawals from your accounts can be most tax-efficient if you are mindful of the differing tax treatments of fully taxable, traditional qualified (e.g., IRA and 401(k) and Roth accounts). We are not tax advisors, so a full discussion of this is beyond our scope. Also, every reader's tax situation can be different, so there is no one-size-fits-all tax strategy. But the following general guidelines can help you plan your envelopes with tax efficiency in mind.

The general principle is: *Defer taxation as long as possible* if you believe your tax rate later will be no higher (and possibly lower) during your retirement than today. That way your accounts grow without the drag, or leakage, of taxes paid each year.

This suggests that for a "typical" smart investor, he or she should spend taxable accounts first, then traditional qualified accounts, and finally Roth accounts. In envelope terms these three spending phases can roughly map into the three envelopes described in this book.

There are numerous caveats; we will name only a few. You will pay a sizable tax penalty if you begin spending from traditional qualified accounts before age 59½, or if you fail to begin taking distributions by age 70½. This clearly suggests relying on taxable accounts before age 59½, and on qualified accounts by no later than age 70½.

In the most general sense, you can allocate accounts with differing tax treatment to envelopes along the following line:

Taxable accounts: Envelopes 1 (primary) and 2 (residual)
Traditional qualified accounts: Envelopes 2 (primary)
    and 3 (residual)
Roth accounts: Envelope 3

This is a *very* simplified guideline, which must be adjusted for your specific circumstances.

A very important proviso: We argue that in the new normal future tax rates are very likely to be much higher than today's. That argues for converting a significant portion of your traditional qualified accounts to Roths. You will pay taxes to convert, but thereafter all growth will be tax-free. Chapter 9 of our earlier book *Your Macroeconomic Edge* covers this in some detail.

Don't Blow the Last Lap

Smart investors like you are in the very distinct minority. You've exercised financial discipline to keep control of your destiny. You aren't hoping for a miracle, or Uncle Sugar Daddy, to bail you out after a lifetime of failure to save.

Now is the time to consolidate your gains, not risk them in pursuit of still more. We know, it is hard to turn a ship that has built up such momentum—to convert from an assiduous accumulator to a smart decumulator. But failure to do so risks all that you spent a lifetime building.

Think of a football analogy: You caught a pass deep in your own territory and have run it 80 yards up the field. Don't start your victory dance until you are actually in the end zone. In baseball terms, don't stop running the bases until you have crossed home plate.

The challenges to smart investors in the next few decades will dwarf those we are accustomed to. When the rules change, so must the playbook. The envelopes approach described here gives you a new playbook for this next stage in your life, and in the life of the global economy. Good luck. If you wish to keep up with our insights as events unfold, or avail yourselves of our help and advice, please visit www.7secretsretirement.com.

Resources

This section includes a sampling of organizations and publications about the topics covered in this book. We have divided them into two sections, one on "the new normal," and the other on "It's the Income, Stupid!"

The New Normal

Agora Publishing

Agora, founded by Bill Bonner, is a holding company that owns a variety of investment and lifestyle-oriented publications. Its flagship is *The Daily Reckoning*, Bonner's witty perspective on financial developments, distributed free by e-mail. http://dailyreckoning.com/

Brookings Institution

Left-of-center counterpart to AEI. Cofounder of the Tax Policy Institute (see following). http://www.brookings.edu/

Bureau of Labor Statistics

The BLS, a bureau of the U.S. Department of Commerce, tabulates and reports a variety of statistics about the labor market, including the unemployment rate. The BLS also maintains the consumer price index (CPI), the bestknown measure of price inflation. http://www.bls.gov/

Council on Foreign Relations, Center for Geoeconomic Studies

Formally known as the Maurice Greenberg Center for Geoeconomic Studies, this arm of the Council on Foreign Relations analyzes trends in the international economy. http://www.cfr.org/thinktank/cgs/

The Economist Magazine

The best general periodical covering the world economy and politics. http://www.economist.com

Financial Times Newspaper

Daily newspaper, published in London, on economic and financial news. Columnist Martin Wolf is a particularly sage commentator on international economics. Gideon Rachman is also highly recommended. http://www.ft.com/home/uk

International Monetary Fund

The IMF, founded at the 1944 Bretton Woods Conference that designed the world's postwar financial order, exists as a lender of last resort for nations in financial difficulty. Its rescue missions are often controversial among recipients of emergency loans, because the discipline the IMF demands as a condition of its loan often aggravates the recipient's condition in the short term. http://www.imf.org/external/index.htm

Peterson Institute for International Economics

Peterson Institute for International Economics, endowed by Peter G. Peterson, is a private, nonprofit, nonpartisan research institution devoted to the study of international economic policy. https://piie.com/

Population Reference Bureau (PRB)

The Population Reference Bureau provides information about population, health, and the environment. A good source of world demographic information. http://www.prb.org/

Rand Corporation

RAND is the original "think tank," founded soon after World War II by the U.S. Air Force to maintain a cadre of civilian scientific advice that had been so useful in wartime. RAND has since diversified well beyond defense to include international demographics. *Full disclosure*: Romero is agraduate of RAND's PhD school. http://www.rand.org/

Stansberry Research

Stansberry & Associates Research publishes a variety of investment newsletters. The *S&A Resources Report* by Matt Badiali focuses on commodities, with an emphasis on energy. Other newsletters have also dealt with looming fiscal challenges and the inflation that will result. http://stansberryresearch.com/

The Wall Street Journal newspaper

The Wall Street Journal is the best United States-based daily for business and economic news. Columnists Greg Ip and Gerald Seib each cover aspects of economic policy. Ip emphasizes the economics and Seib the politics. Jason Zweig writes a personal finance/investing column. http://www.wsj.com/

World Bank

Known formally as the International Bank of Reconstruction and Development, the World Bank originated at Bretton Woods to provide long-term financing to nations rebuilding after World War II. Today, the World Bank acts as a multilateral international aid facilitator and financier, with emphasis on aid to developing nations. http://www.worldbank.org/

Retirement Planning and the Income/Envelopes Approach

The literature on personal finance and retirement is vast. Here we mention only a few sources that we believe share our perspective about the importance of subdividing your portfolio by time horizon. We call this approach "envelopes"; others call it "baskets" or "buckets." Also included are a few sources of valuable macro information on trends in the retiree population and its challenges, including savings and pension trends.

Center for Retirement Research at Boston College

This center "promote(s) research on retirement issues, to transmit new findings to the policy community and the public, to help train new scholars, and to broaden access to valuable data sources." Excellent source for studies about retirement trends and policies. http://crr.bc.edu/

Joe Hearn, Intentional Retirement

Hearn is a financial planner who takes a holistic perspective on retirement, viewing it as an exciting life stage. He emphasizes nonfinancial aspects at least as much as the more common emphasis on savings and finance. www.intentionalretirement.com

Kiplinger's Magazine

A competitor of *Money* magazine. For when you've passed through the introductory phase of personal financial planning. http://www.kiplinger.com/

MetLife Mature Market Institute (MMI)

MMI is MetLife's research organization, emphasizing the multidimensional and multigenerational issues of aging and longevity. https://www.metlife.com/mmi/index.html

Moshe Milvesky

This York University finance professor is author of a number of very accessible books on retirement and financial planning. His recent work has focused on annuities as an important component of retirement portfolios. http://milevsky.info.yorku.ca/

Money Magazine

A good layman's introduction to personal finance issues, including budgeting; saving for college, a home, or retirement; and investing. http://time.com/money/

Morgan Stanley

Researchers at this firm bank have studied the performance of portfolios segmented by time horizon ("envelopes" to us, "time baskets" to them). We reported on the results of their back-testing in Chapter 6. http://www.morganstanley.com/

Charles Reinhard, Nicholas Richard, and Zi Ye, Putting Investors' Eggs in Separate Time Baskets, June 2010. http://sanddollar-invest.com/pdfs/SeparateTimeBaskets.pdf

Morningstar

Morningstar is a highly regarded clearinghouse of information on mutual funds. Personal finance director Christine Benz has published and spoken extensively about the envelopes framework. http://www.morningstar.com/

National Inflation Association

The NIA is a new organization "dedicated to preparing Americans for hyperinflation. While many of its transmissionsemphasize investment advice (for a fee), it is a valuable clearinghouse forinformation on how to protect against a phenomenon many baby boomers have not considered. There is some indication that NIA exists mainly to promote certain investments. Buyer beware. http://www.inflation.us

Other Research Into the Role of Annuities in the Envelopes Approach

The above sources are seminal, but many more authors have produced valuable information on topics related to this book. Annuities in particular have generated significant scrutiny and disagreement, as Chapter 16 noted. Below is a sampling of some of the more recent studies on the merits of these complex and controversial products.

Author(s)	Article	Publication	Date
Bauer, Kling and Russ	A universal pricing framework for guaranteed minimum benefits in variable annuities	*ASTIN Bulletin*	2008
Benartzi & Thaler	Annuitization puzzles	*Journal of Economic Perspectives*	2011
Blanchett	Optimal portfolio allocations with GMWB annuities	*Journal of Financial Planning*	2012
Blanchett	Low Bond Yields and Efficient Retirement Income Portfolios	*The Journal of Retirement*	2013
Chang, DeJong, Liu, and Robinson	The Cost of Guaranteed Income: Demystifying the Value Proposition of Variable Annuities with GLWB Riders	*Retirement Management Journal*	2014
Kitces & Pfau	The True Impact of Immediate Annuities on Retirement Sustainability: A Total Wealth Perspective	*Retirement Management Journal*	2014
Dai, Kwok, & Zong	Guaranteed minimum withdrawal benefits in variable annuities	*Mathematical Finance*	2008
Huang Grove & Taylor	The Efficient Income Frontier: A Product Allocation Framework for Retirement	*Retirement Management Journal*	2012
Milevsky & Kyrychenko	Portfolio choice with puts: Evidence from variable annuities	*Financial Analysts Journal*	2008
Robinson	A context for considering variable annuities with contemporary living benefit riders	*Journal of Financial Planning*	2008
Steinorth & Mitchell	Valuing variable annuities with guaranteed minimum lifetime withdrawal benefits	*Pension Research Council*	2012
Xion, Idzorek and Chen	Allocation to deferred variable annuities with GMWB for life	*Journal of Financial Planning*	2010